the Spunky Coconut cookbook

GLUTEN FREE • CASEIN FREE • SUGAR FREE

KELLY V. BROZYNA

Book design by AJB Design, Inc. www.ajbdesign.com

This book is intended as a source of information only. The text and recipes should not be considered a substitute for professional medical expertise. The author disclaims any liability for any adverse effects arising from the application of the information found herein. The reader should consult a qualified health professional before starting any new diet or health program.

ISBN-10: 1-4392-3576-7
ISBN-13: 978-14392-3576-8
Library of Congress Control Number: 2009903199

To my husband, Andrew
and my girls, Zoe + Ashley

Contents

Introduction 1

Safe Cooking & Storage 5

Green Your Home...7

Avoiding Sugar..9

Why Use Coconut Oil 12

Lemon Juice for Acid Reflux 12

Oxalates 13

Appliances and Products...14

The Recipes

Smoothies & Shakes 19

Nut Milk & Pudding 28

Bread & Muffins 34

Ice Cream...47

Pumpkin Cookin' 59

Cakes & Brownies..62

Salad & Appetizers 81

Quiche & Casserole 98

Pasta...107

Soup 114

Sides 123

Meat 133

Pie & Cheesecake 141

Cookies & Treats..150

Recommended Reading...175

Metric Conversion Tables 176

Index 177

Introduction

In my home we are successfully treating a slew of modern epidemics, from autism and ADD, to celiac disease and gluten-intolerance. These terms, which we use to label our physical and behavioral problems, are environmentally triggered, both by the food that we eat, and the toxins we are exposed to from conception. Therefore, the key to solving our problems is changing our diet, adding supplements, excreting toxins, and avoiding further toxic exposures.

In the early 1980's one in 10,000 children had autism. In the year 2009 there are one in every 150 children with autism. We know that there is no such thing as a purely genetic epidemic, but it is clear that many of our children have a predisposition, *which is environmentally triggered*. This predisposition is the inability to excrete toxins. Why wasn't this inability to excrete toxins triggered as often in the past? The answer is because in the last 30 years the amount of toxins in our environment has drastically increased. When toxins are present in our bodies, a host of other problems are created, such as depleted levels of glutathione (our bodies natural toxin eliminator), the overgrowth of systemic yeast, as well as other GI issues, and the presence of viruses and bacteria.

One toxic exposure that we must refuse is the injection of poisons into our babies. I doubt if any of you have not been privy to Jenny McCarthy's very public coming-out, so to speak, on vaccine ingredients and the insane increase in the number of shots given in recent years. The fact of the matter, as Jenny and Jim express, is that vaccines contain mercury, aluminum, antifreeze, and formaldehyde. They also point out that the number of vaccines given has increased from 10 in 1983 to 36 currently, while no independent studies have proven this quantity and combination to be safe. (See GenerationRescue.org for unbiased research.)

Since our youngest daughter nearly died from seizures the evening of her 4 month vaccine reaction, I have had several friends go to their unknowing pediatricians who denied the presence of mercury, aluminum, antifreeze, and formaldehyde in *their* vaccines. Obviously, certain doctor's offices are not being granted special toxin-free vaccines – *come on people!* For this reason, you have to make your own decision (Yes you do have a choice! And they can still go to public school with a vaccine exemption in every state!), before going to the pediatrician, or find DAN! doctors who don't pressure vaccines, as we have done. (http://www.vaclib.org/exemption.htm)

I have come to realize that parents who go to the pediatrician uncertain are simply looking to be reassured that vaccines are safe and effective. Yet, the fact of the matter is that most pediatricians are uneducated on vaccines, though they would never admit it. If, however, vaccines were safe and effective, then I'm sure pediatricians would have no problem signing an acceptance of responsibility form (as opposed to their zero liability waiver which the parent is asked to sign), before injecting your baby with mercury, aluminum, antifreeze and formaldehyde. <http://www.knowshots.com>

Gluten and Casein

Now that prevention of poisoning is out of the way lets talk about reversing damage that is already done. There are several books, which I highly recommend such as Children With Starving Brains, Healing the New Childhood Epidemics, and Louder Than Words. These books discuss treatments, which are proven effective, like essential fatty acids, probiotics, enzymes, certain vitamins, detoxification, and of course the gluten-free/casein-free/sugar-free diet.

Gluten is the protein in wheat, spelt, barley, contaminated oats, and rye. Casein is the protein in dairy. Gluten and casein are almost identical on a molecular level. People with compromised intestines, or leaky gut, have perforations in their GI tracts which allow partially digested food to escape into the blood stream, where it makes it's way to the brain. Gluten and casein proteins attach to receptors in the brain in a similar way as opiates. In a manner of speaking, gluten and casein can create the effect of being on drugs.

For children susceptible to autism this leads to behavior such as screaming, violence, repetitive actions, hyperactivity, being "lost in their own world", etc. When my daughter, Ashley, was "on dairy," as we say in my house, she would freak out as if hallucinating, and for all I know, maybe she was. Ashley has never had gluten, and when she became free of casein she stopped opening and closing drawers for hours at a time, banging her head on the floor and wall, flapping and screaming.

Since we removed dairy from Ashley's diet there have been a few times when she has accidentally come into contact with it. Each time she has regressed into severe autism within minutes. Once it happened on the way to a friend's house, when I gave her a bar that I thought was safe. In the time it took to drive the short distance, Ashley started freaking out. She had that wild look in her eyes, she was shrieking and flapping her hands, her arms raised like they would float away. Inside my friend's house, I read the wrapper and found the culprit: dairy. I remember my friend looking at Ashley's behavior and saying to me, "I'm so sorry. It must be so hard for you." All I could say was, "She isn't usually like this." We left shortly thereafter because it was impossible for us to talk over Ashley's episode, and I just had to leave, almost in tears. A few hours later, when it was out of her system, she was back to herself again, just like that.

When my husband was on gluten and dairy he experienced ADD. For years when we were dating and first married I could hardly talk to him at times because he couldn't focus on what I was saying. It was like trying to carry on a conversation with a zombie. He was also extremely forgetful and had terrible gas. It was frustrating for him, and it was also hard on me. I'm so glad that he has seen how being gluten and casein free has completely taken away his ADD and gas. He chooses the diet over the side effects he experiences on gluten and dairy.

Before I discovered that I had celiac disease I was so constipated. I pooped about once a week for most of my life, and I thought this was normal. When I was a child the doctor told my mother to give me prunes. I remember eating them while crying on the toilet. In college I went through a period where I had constant pain, and would wake up in the middle of the night throwing up. A doctor guessed I had a stomach ulcer so he advised I drink milk (which only made matters worse of course), and prescribed medication. Years later when I had diarrhea for three months straight, and lost 30 pounds, a different doctor assumed I had a parasite, and without proof gave me enough antibiotics for an elephant.

Now that I am gluten and casein free I no longer have constipation, diarrhea, pain or vomit. Someone once said that doctors would diagnose celiac disease if they had a pill for it. Although awareness is growing, most doctors still use the grossly inaccurate blood test. EnteroLab, on the other hand, is the most progressive test to date. They have stool and genetic tests, both of which are non-invasive, and don't require a referral, although all of our DAN! doctors recommend them. (https://www.enterolab.com)

People sometimes feel sorry for us that we don't eat gluten, dairy, or sugar, but I always tell them it's so worth it! Many parents I know have chosen to follow this diet rather than make two meals at a time, and some adults, like my husband and I, have found that they need to eat this way as much as their children do! My goal over the years became creating food that was so good that no one would ever know or care it was free of gluten, casein, and sugar. The more I studied nutrition with my doctor of naturopathy, the more our diets changed. We now eat organic, local, and fair trade as much as possible. We also gave up artificial flavors, coloring, preservatives, and nitrates.

I remember when I was just in high school, and my friend, Serela, told me that what matters most in life is health. She was only 16 at the time. What can I say? She was wise for her years!

Cheers to your good health!

Safe Cooking and Storage

Safe cooking

Aluminum and non-stick coating transfer toxins into your food as you cook. In the interest of keeping your family healthy it's best to use cast iron, iron coated in enamel or ceramics. If you use stainless steel, just make sure that you flip with a plastic spatula or stir with a plastic spoon, because banging another metal against stainless releases unwanted metals like nickel into your food.

Safe storage

Just as aluminum (foil as well as pots and pans) and non-stick surfaces transfer toxins to your food when you cook with them, storing your food and drinks in plastic or polycarbonates transfer toxins as well. Therefore, to avoid toxins from leaching into your food and drinks it's best to use glass or ceramics storage containers, both in the pantry and the refrigerator. In addition to leaching toxins, plastics hold odors, stain, and break, meaning that you constantly need to replace them, and making them a bad choice for the environment.

In order to save energy and money we collect and re-use glass jars from products we buy. Vegenaise Grapeseed Oil and ghee jars are two of our favorites.

To drink safely when we're out and about we use SIGG™ bottles. SIGG™ bottles are made from aluminum, but coated on the inside with enamel so there are no toxins leaching into your water. Another reason to use them is that, "Americans add over 30 million plastic bottles to our nations landfills—*everyday!*" SIGG™ bottles are good for the environment because they are reusable, no more plastic bottles necessary. They can also be recycled if after a few years you decide to buy another one.

When I pack a lunch for Andrew and I, I use a kind of recycled plastic called Preserve® by Recycline, Inc. These containers are much heavier and more durable than their non-environmentally friendly plastic competitors, and they don't use #6 polystyrene plastic. Because they are 100% recycled and recyclable they save energy and natural resources, plus they are made in the USA, reducing fuel and maintaining a smaller footprint.

It is estimated that on average a school-age child using a disposable lunch generates 67 pounds of waste per school year. This isn't limited to disposable bags, but individually wrapped snacks like chips and cookies, plastic bags for sandwiches and carrots, paper napkins, foil and plastic silverware too. Approximately 18,760 pounds of lunch waste is accumulated for just one average-size elementary school. This is why Zoe and Ashley use bento boxes from Laptop Lunches™ <http://www.laptoplunches.com> when they pack a lunch. These bento boxes are lead-free, BPA-free, and they create waste free lunches <http://www.wastefreelunches.org>.

Green Your Home

When we say we need to save the environment, what we are also saying is we need to protect the future of the human race. Global warming is taking effect on humans with disasters like hurricane Katrina in Louisiana, Dolly and Ike in Texas. We have to change our habits now, or these kinds of events will only increase as they have been. (*The 11th Hour*, Leonardo DiCaprio)

In addition to voting, there is a lot you can do for the environment at home. You can start by substituting petroleum-based products with plant based biodegradable dish soap, dish washing detergent, and laundry detergent. Seventh Generation™ states, "If every household in the US replaced just one box of 42 load petroleum based powder laundry detergent with our plant based product, **we could save 238,000 barrels of oil**, enough to heat and cool **13,600 US homes for a year**!" That is awesome!

Another way we conserve is by using cloth dish towels and cloth diapers rather than paper towels and paper diapers (which are coated in plastic and full of perfumes and deodorant). Based on a report from the Women's Environmental Network, The Real Diaper Association, reports:

- Disposable diapers are the third most common consumer product in landfills today.

- A disposable diaper may take up to 500 years to decompose.

- One baby in disposable diapers will contribute at least 1 ton of waste to your local landfill.

We love Fuzzi Bunz™ cloth diapers in our house. You just have to make sure to get a snug fit. For inserts we choose hemp, which is incredibly absorbent, and good for the environment. We also add one cotton insert, for a total of 4 layers. In all our years of using them we have had no more accidents than others using disposables. However, as we parents know, having babies isn't easy or convenient, but it's so worth it, and so are the choices we make for the planet and the future of mankind.

You can also choose, as we have, to buy a high efficiency front-loading washer and dryer, which use 70 percent less water and 70 percent less energy! Isn't that exciting?

You can save money and protect the environment at the same time! Just make sure to use HE (high efficiency) designed detergent, like Seventh Generation™.

Finally, carry these ideas over into cleaning your kitchen and bathroom. There are a ton of environmentally friendly household cleaners out there. Have fun researching them and finding your own favorite. Share your discoveries with your friends and family. In our home we make cleaning spray with a mixture of peroxide and water. It's inexpensive, and we refill the same spray bottle every time, so there is less consumption and waste.

Avoiding Sugar

Why avoid sugar?

Many consider sugar, as we know it today, to be poison. This is because the most common forms of sugar are refined. The refining process removes natural vitamins and minerals so that the sugar becomes depleted. To correct this problem our bodies pull vitamins and minerals from within. "For example: to protect the blood, calcium is drawn from the bones and teeth, so much in fact that it tends to weaken and decay the bones. This precipitates osteoarthritis. Refined sugar in the diet can damage the digestive tract and over time every organ in the body."[1]

It is also well established that sugar causes hypoglycemia and leads to obesity, diabetes, high blood pressure and bad cholesterol, which increases chances of heart disease. Plus, sugar triggers autoimmune disorders like allergies, asthma, arthritis, and MS, and feeds the growth of cancer cells.

Another big reason why my family doesn't use refined sugar is because sugar feeds yeast. Every DAN! doctor will tell you that one of the largest obstacles in our children's spectrum disorders is the battle against systemic yeast. My friends and I call them, "the yeasty-beasties." There are two main causes of systemic yeast overgrowth—lack of good bacteria passed through birth and obtained thereafter, and overuse of antibiotics. Once yeast becomes rampant, it is incredibly difficult to get rid of, partially because yeast feeds on sugar in the diet.

Natural Alternatives to Refined Sugar

STEVIA

This is our stevia plant. Isn't it cute? We haven't sun dried or dehydrated any leaves, and don't plan to, because it's so incredibly sweet straight off the plant. The green leaves taste like a cross between an apple and a honeysuckle. Unfortunately, it's too small to really use yet. We want to make sure it's really established before plucking away at it. My husband, Andrew, grew it from a seed.

---

1   <http://www.ghchealth.com/refined-sugar.html>

When we moved to Colorado Andrew carefully placed three baby stevia plants in a dish that fit exactly into the cup-holder of our car. He also packed his Mac, and some important papers, along with our Boston Terrier, Cherry, and Persian cat, Tiger. Then, he and his younger sister, drove across the country. It took them three days at about 10 hours of driving a day. The girls and I flew into Denver, after they arrived, where we were reunited.

A while after moving into our apartment, two of the three plants died. This is our only surviving stevia plant. It's now a year and a half old.

I've read a bit about the stevia controversy, and I don't find it the least bit hard to believe that the FDA removed the Generally Regarded As Safe (GRAS) label of stevia to benefit the American artificial sweetener industry. In the 1980s a company complained to the FDA that a tea sold by Celestial Seasonings™ contained the stevia sweetener. The FDA memorandum is available under the Freedom of Information Act, yet the company name of the complainant has been removed to protect their identity.[2] In 1993 Arizona Congressman Jon Kyl wrote a letter to FDA Commissioner David Kessler regarding the 1991 stevia import ban. He asserted that the FDA's restriction of stevia was "a restraint of trade to benefit the artificial sweetener industry"[3] Stevia has continued to be available in this country, yet it must be labeled as an "herbal supplement" not a "sweetener." In 2008 the first available stevia sweetener for foods and beverages was released. The FDA approved Rebaudioside A, the stevia-derived chemical in the TRUVIA™ sweetener, whereas the stevia plant itself (or any other chemical derived from it) remains barred from use as a food additive. Why was TRUVIA™ awarded GRAS status, while other Stevia products remain in the herbal supplement aisle? Once again, it seems to be the influence of American big business. TRUVIA™ was developed by The Coca-Cola Company and Cargill—both US companies.

---

2   Hawke, Jenny. "The Bittersweet Story of the Stevia Herb," found in *Nexus Magazine*, Volume 10, Number 2 (February–March 2003).
    A transcript of this article can be seen on <http://www.whale.to/b/hawke.html>

3   *Stevia: Quotes And Comments By Researchers*, Herbal Remedies USA LLC, viewed January, 16 2009, <http://www.herbalremedies.com/stevquotandc.html>

Stevia is very low on the glycemic index, making it suitable for diabetics, or anyone who doesn't want to spike their blood sugar or eat refined [depleted] sugar. Some day I plan on using our stevia leaves in my food, but in the meantime I will continue buying it at the health food store or on Amazon.com.

Stevia comes in powder and liquid form. Both the powder and the liquid are very concentrated, meaning you only need a tiny bit. Stevia costs more up-front, but saves you money in the long run because it lasts so long. As you can tell from my recipes I am particularly fond of the liquid stevia. I would say it's the key ingredient in my baked goods.

XYLITOL

Xylitol is rendered from the fibers of fruits and vegetables. Like stevia, it is very low on the glycemic index, so it doesn't spike blood sugar levels, and is therefore suitable for diabetics as well as the health-conscious. Unlike stevia, which tends to taste like diet in drinks, xylitol does not have any aftertaste. It dissolves nicely into hot tea and coffee, sweetening wonderfully. However, it is best to have xylitol with food, because it can cause diarrhea on an empty stomach. I use xylitol in my cooking where I feel it is more appropriate than stevia, honey or agave. Xylitol's sweetness is less concentrated than stevia and more concentrated than refined white sugar. For example, one cup of refined white sugar is roughly equivalent to one quarter cup of xylitol or one teaspoon of stevia powder. What is also interesting about xylitol is that it greatly reduces plaque and cavities.

Note: Always be careful to keep food and supplements (like Zyme Prime™) away from your dog or other pets. While perfectly safe for people, xylitol is deadly for pets.

AGAVE

Agave nectar or syrup comes from the agave plant—the same plant used in tequila. Like stevia and xylitol, agave is low on the glycemic index. It looks much like honey, though it is less viscous. Agave also has a less distinct flavor than honey when used in food and drinks, which makes it my favorite choice for coffee. Although it is 90% fructose, agave differs from crystalline fructose, which is most often refined from corn, and contains processing chemicals.

Why Use Coconut Oil

You will notice that the only oil I use in my cooking is coconut oil, for which there are some very good reasons.

Oils like sesame, sunflower, flax and even olive oil are very healthy when raw, but highly likely to undergo oxidative damage when cooked because they contain polyunsaturated fats. The heating of oils, which contain unsaturated fat, creates damaged molecules. Dr. Mercola calls these "toxic fats." Coconut oil is almost entirely saturated fat, which makes it the safest choice for heating.[4]

Additionally, coconut oil is a medium-chain fat. This means that we are able to convert the fat in coconut oil to energy, rather than storing it in the body as fat. Coconut oil is also 40 percent lauric acid. The only other source of lauric acid comes from human breast milk. Lauric acid is extremely beneficial to your immune system. It is incredibly antibacterial and antiviral. Lauric acid is the reason why breast-fed babies have greatly reduced illness and infections.[5]

Lemon Juice for Acid Reflux

An alkaline diet is the best prevention for acid reflux, but there is also a less well-known secret to treating acid reflux. Lemon juice. Drinking a glass of lemon water first thing in the morning, and before meals is a great way to prevent acid reflux. Lemon juice neutralizes acids and provides an alkaline environment. In addition to prevention, lemon juice can also be taken straight when symptoms are present, to tighten the sphincter muscle, which allows acid to ascend into the esophagus.

---

4   Mercola, Joseph. PhD. <http://www.mercola.com/> Viewed on January 16, 2009.
5   Fife, Bruce. N.D. "Coconut Oil and Medium-Chain Triglycerides" Coconut Research Center. Viewed on January 16, 2009. <http://www.coconutresearchcenter.org/article10612.htm>

Oxalates

It seems like all the most nutritious foods are also high in oxalic acid, an acid that can form crystals in the body, which irritate the gut and kidneys. Dark greens, nuts and berries are among my favorite high oxalate foods. When our daughter, Ashley, wasn't excreting oxalates it caused her a lot of pain, especially at night. It was so bad that I actually put her on the low oxalate diet for a year. She started sleeping better immediately. I gradually added high oxalate foods back into her diet by giving her extra calcium citrate. Calcium citrate bonds with oxalates, so they can be excreted.

It's very obvious when Ashley has had too many high oxalate foods and not enough calcium citrate because she gets excessive thirst. The first time this happened I didn't make the connection between the oxalates and the thirst, and she woke up every hour that night, arching her back in pain. Now I give her more calcium citrate at the first sign of excessive thirst, and it takes care of it right away. However, we avoid reaching that point 90 percent of the time just by staying consistent with the calcium citrate every day.

Since we give Ashley enzymes with every meal, we just mix the calcium citrate right in. My husband got a nice little mortar and pestle, which we use to grind Zyme Prime™ chewable tabs, by Houston Nutraceuticals, Inc. We do this because Ashley doesn't like to chew or swallow vitamins and enzymes. We grind a handful at a time and keep the powder in a glass jar in the vitamin cabinet. Mixing the Zyme Prime™ and the calcium citrate (Cal/Mag Citrate, by New Beginnings Nutritionals) works well because the enzymes have a nice berry flavor which covers up the cal/mag. We use applesauce to mix the two together, and she eats it from a spoon. It actually tastes pretty good.

Appliances and Products

My recipes are not difficult, however, you do need some quality appliances and a few of my staple products, like SweetLeaf™ Liquid Stevia.

STEVIA

Vanilla Crème, Chocolate Raspberry, Cinnamon, and English Toffee by SweetLeaf™ are the flavors you will find in this book. They are commonly sold at local health food stores, but if your's doesn't carry it, most local places will order them for you if you ask. They can also be found at larger chains like Whole Foods, Wegmans, Vitamin Cottage and Trader Joes, or on SweetLeaf.com. Flavored liquid stevia is the key ingredient in my baked goods.

COCONUT OIL

The coconut oil I use comes from Tropical Traditions. I buy it from the company website by the gallon to cut down on cost <http://www.tropicaltraditions.com>. I've also combined orders with friends to save on shipping and to get better deals. We've been using coconut oil long enough now that we can't taste the coconut anymore. However, flavorless coconut oil is also available.

GHEE

Although this clarified butter is considered dairy, ghee is free of casein and lactose, and it gives you that buttery taste.

BLENDER

In order to properly blend and to keep up with daily use it's really important to get a professional blender like a Blendtec™ or a Vita-Mix™.

FOOD PROCESSOR

When I'm not using my blender I'm making a crust or a dip using my food processor. The one we own is the Cuisinart Prep 11 Plus™. Like my blender, I couldn't be happier with my food processor.

DEHYDRATOR

For dehydrating I use the second best dehydrator, the Nesco American Harvest™. It's only second behind the Excalibur™ dehydrators because of the tubular design, which limits the size of your recipes slightly. However, my Nesco™ was just over half the cost of the least expensive Excalibur™, and it works extremely well. Dehydrating is such a great option for making healthy, nutritious cookies and snack bars. Several of my recipes are made in the dehydrator.

ICE CREAM MACHINE

I highly recommend purchasing an ice cream machine if you don't already have one. Ice cream may sound unnecessary, but it's a major food group in our house! My ice cream recipes are so healthy and nutritious that I prefer my kids eat ice cream over packaged gluten-free cereal for breakfast. We own a Cuisinart 1½ Quart Automatic Ice Cream Maker. It's awesome!

BEEF GELATIN

Beef gelatin is very healing to the gut, and when added to nut milks it creates such a creamy ice cream. Unless you are vegetarian I hope you will try my technique. Otherwise, ½ tsp of xanthan gum can be substituted. I recommend beef gelatin by Now® Foods, which can be found in the health food store, as well as online.

XANTHAN GUM

Xanthan gum is great for adding a gluten-like texture to a recipe. Its production typically involves corn, but Now® Foods sells a corn-free alternative.

If you prefer to use the internet—as I do—all of these products and appliances can be found on Amazon.com and elsewhere.

The Recipes

Chocolate Shake

Add to blender:

²/₃ cup chocolate mousse
(see p. 31)

10 ice cubes

1 to 2 tsp cocoa
or cacao powder

2 squirts of agave

enough almond milk to just
get it going in the blender

Purée.

Optional:

2 tbsp Vitol Egg
Protein Powder

Those who like decadent desserts will call me crazy, but I actually prefer a chocolate shake over chocolate mousse! The texture of a smoothie or shake just really appeals to me. There is something comforting about it, and really American too. I think of the diner scene in the movie *Grease*.

I also love when a dish becomes something else, like this chocolate shake made with my chocolate mousse. You would never guess what it was made of. It's so healthy we drink it for breakfast.

Mint Shake

Add to blender:

8–10 fresh
spearmint leaves

6 frozen vanilla pudding
cubes *(see p. 31)*

3 ice cubes

3 drops Vanilla Crème
liquid stevia

1 tsp raw honey

¾ cup almond milk
(see p. 29)

a few drops of
lemon juice

I got this idea into my head that I wanted to make
a green shake, using fresh spearmint leaves. When
I found a spearmint plants outside at Whole Foods,
I was set. It came out this celadon green color that
was so pretty. You can also try throwing in some
dairy-free chocolate chips, and give them a quick
spin, so you get that chocolate fleck effect.

Nutcracker Sweet® Tea Latté

Add to blender:

9 cubes of frozen cashew milk *(see p. 30)*

1 tbsp honey

10 drops Vanilla Crème liqiud stevia

2 cups chilled Nutcracker Sweet® holiday tea by Celestial Seasonings™

a dash of cinnamon or pumpkin pie spice

Purée.

Makes one serving.

You could also spike this a little and serve it to company at a holiday party. Yum!

I wasn't really crazy about this tea when it was hot, but chilled and blended with frozen cashew milk it is *incredibly delicious*. Like, I want to go make another one right now just thinking about it, delicious. If you got something like this at the coffee shop they would rob you of 4 dollars, delicious. You've gotta try it.

Purple Pear Smoothies

Add to blender:

1 packet frozen Sambazon® Pure Acai smoothie pack

1 cup frozen blueberries

2 cups frozen strawberries

¼ cup honey or agave

1 tsp vanilla extract

1 cup 100% pear juice*

1 cup water (or 2 cups pear juice and no water, depending on how pear-tasting you like it)

Purée.

I use R.W. Knudsen.

I am constantly trying to invent new smoothies, scouring the freezer aisle and reading raw food books for inspiration. I do it partly because I am obsessed with smoothies, really I could live on them, and partly because I love the convenience of smoothies. They make a great breakfast or afternoon snack, or both if you're me! This one, has a glorious deep purple color, yet a surprising pear taste. My oldest, Zoe, loves it, and she is the pickiest, even when it comes to smoothies.

Chocolate Banana Shake

Add to blender:

1 frozen banana
(freeze in pieces)

6 cubes of frozen Vanilla
Pudding *(see p. 31)*

1 cup almond
or cashew milk *(see p. 30)*

1 tsp honey or agave

1 tbsp cocoa
or cacao powder

a dash of cinnamon

Purée.

This shake tastes just like a creamy dairy milk shake. *sigh*... It's like you and I have the secret to a beautiful dairy-free existence—nuts! No, not "nuts" like "darn," nuts like cashews and almonds—those nuts! Now if only I could get someone to pick me up for my own line of (dairy-free) nut milk ice cream. How do you go about doing that? I don't know, oh well... Enjoy the shake!

Cherry Smoothies

Add to blender:

4 cups frozen
organic cherries

a squirt of agave and/or a
few drops of Vanilla Crème
liquid stevia

3 tbsp Vitol Egg Protein
Powder

almond milk to just cover
the cherries in the blender

Purée.

We make smoothies nearly every morning, and this is the one we make most often. I think I speak for all of us when I say we just can't get enough of them!

Power Smoothies

Add to blender:

1½ cups frozen cherries

½ banana

1 tsp honey

½ tsp Acai Berry Emergen-C®

2 tbsp Vanilla Vitol Egg Protein Powder

1 cup orange juice

1 cup almond milk *(see p. 29)*

Purée.

The name says it all! This smoothie is a powerhouse of nutrition, and it tastes fabulous too!

Blueberry Cream Smoothies

Add to blender:

2 cups frozen blueberries

4 cubes of frozen Vanilla Pudding *(see p. 31)*

1 tbsp honey or agave

1 tsp vanilla extract

Purée with enough almond milk or cashew milk to just get it going.

Optional:

2 tbsp Vitol Egg Protein Powder—Energized with Bee Pollen. Enzyme activated with Papain and Bromelain. Plus that great creamy flavor!

When we lived on the east coast I remember thinking how the summers in Colorado must be like they are in Maine. One of my good childhood friends moved to Maine when we were still young, and twice we went to visit her, since our moms are also close. It was so much cooler there in the summer than where we lived in Maryland. In Maryland it was so humid and hot that we hardly ever went outside in the summer. I thought Colorado was going to be like Maine, but it actually gets very hot in the Front Range, minus the humidity. These blueberry cream smoothies are a favorite of ours on hot summer days.

Frozen Café au Lait

Add to blender:

1½ ice cube trays of frozen cashew milk
(see p. 30)

12 drops Vanilla Crème liquid stevia

¼ cup honey or agave

Pour refrigerated coffee over the cubes up to the number 4 cup line. Blend.

For a seasonal twist add a dash of pumpkin pie spice.

If you are casein-free like me and you haven't made cashew milk yet, please do! I don't like cashews, but cashew milk is delicious, and it makes a great substitute for cream, like in my dairy-free frozen café au lait. I used to envy my friends with their coffee shop frozen cappuccinos, but no longer! When I get that yearning I just come home and whip up one of these. Feeling deprived is a thing of the past.

All of my shakes, smoothies and ice creams contain at least one of the ingredients in this section, and so do many of my other recipes. Making your own fresh nut milk is more beneficial to your health, better for the environment than packaged, and saves you money. It seems as though at any given moment you can find raw nuts soaking on my counter!

Nuts contain an enzyme inhibitor, which makes them hard to digest. By soaking them, and rinsing them well in fresh water, you are removing this enzyme inhibitor. This makes them easier to digest, and gives your body access to all the nutrition available in nuts. Once you make nut milk a few times, and see how quick and easy it is, you'll never buy packaged dairy substitute again!

Here is a photo of how I store my nut milks in the refrigerator—almond, cashew, hemp, coconut, etc. I like to use glass because plastic leaches toxins into your food and drinks. Also glass doesn't hold odors or stain like plastic. You can find jugs like these on Amazon.com.

Nut Milk + Pudding

Almond Milk

Blend:

 1 cup blanched almonds

 4–5 cups purified water

Strain through nut milk bag.

Add a few tbsp agave.

Don't throw away the almond solids left in the nut milk bag! You can make cookies (p. 150 & 156)!

I make almond milk by blending a cup of blanched almonds with 4 to 5 cups of purified water, and straining it through a nut milk bag. You can buy nut milk bags online. I get mine from Amazon.com. Or, you can also use cheesecloth. Add a few tablespoons of agave for sweetness. A little vanilla is also really nice in almond milk. *Almonds, like cashews and other nuts/seeds should be stored in the refrigerator.*

Almonds are high in protein, fiber, calcium, magnesium, potassium, vitamin E, natural enzymes and antioxidants. Additionally, almonds help prevent osteoporosis and they regulate blood pressure. They also lower bad cholesterol and reduce risk of heart disease.

Nut Milk + Pudding

Cashew Milk

Soak 1 cup plain cashews overnight. *Not roasted or seasoned.*

Rinse in a bowl of fresh water, strain and repeat several times.

Add to blender:

1 cup soaked cashews

4 cups of purified water

¼ cup agave or honey

1 tsp vanilla extract

Purée.

This is not meant to be stained though a nut milk bag, as with almond milk.

Cashews are a significant source of iron, magnesium (promotes energy release and bone growth), phosphorus (builds bones and teeth), zinc (essential to digestion and metabolism) and selenium (has important antioxidant properties, thus protecting the body from cancer). They are also a good source of protein. Cashews should be stored in the refrigerator.

Hemp Milk

Add to blender:

¼ cup shelled hemp seeds and fill with water up to the 3 cup line

Purée. Strain through nut milk bag if necessary.

Add:

3 tbsp agave

1 tsp vanilla extract

Hemp milk is full of essential fatty acids (omega-3 and omega-6), calcium, iron, and 5 grams of protein per tablespoon! Make sure to store the seeds in the refrigerator.

Vanilla Pudding

Add to food processor:

½ cup cashews, soaked for at least three hours, rinsed and drained

½ cup coconut oil, liquefied

Process for a few minutes, until it looks like nut butter

Add:

¼ cup agave or honey

1 tbsp vanilla extract

½ to ¾ cup whole coconut milk

Process for a couple minutes.

To set:

Pour into a dish and refrigerate for at least 5 hours

The less coconut milk you put in, the thicker the pudding will become. Freeze in ice cube trays for making smoothies and shakes.

Chocolate Mousse

Follow Vanilla Pudding recipe (above), but use:

1 cup *whole* coconut milk

2 to 4 tbsp cocoa powder or cacao powder, depending on how dark you want it

Whipped Topping

Add to blender:

1 can coconut milk (not "lite"), I use organic Thai Kitchen®

1 tbsp vanilla extract

3 tbsp xylitol

5 drops English Toffee liquid stevia

1 tsp xanthan gum

Blend.

CHOCOLATE VARIATION

Same as above except...

½ tsp xanthan gum
Instead of 1 tsp.

plus 1½ tbsp cocoa or cacao powder

Like magic, this simple whipped topping sets up right in your blender. It can be used right away or saved in the refrigerator for later. It will be even thicker after it's cold. I eat it with fresh sliced banana or add it to a piece of cake.

Interestingly, I have tried this recipe with nut milks like cashew and almond, and neither created the same whipped-like results.

Pumpkin Muffins

Add dry ingredients to a bowl:

½ cup tapioca flour

¾ coconut flour, sifted

¼ brown rice flour

½ tsp xanthan gum

1 tsp baking soda

1 tsp baking powder

3 tsp pumpkin pie spice

¼ tsp sea salt

Add to another bowl:

1 tsp vanilla extract

1/8 tsp of cinnamon
liquid stevia

⅔ cup honey or agave

1 cup coconut oil, liquefied

4 room temp eggs (cold
eggs would solidify the
coconut oil)

1½ cups pumpkin

Beat with electric mixer.

**Add dry ingredients
and beat again.**

Optional:

1 cup raisins or
chopped walnuts

**Bake at 350° F for about 20
minutes.**

*The batter will be dry, but the
muffins will become light and fluffy.*

Zucchini Bread

Set oven to 350° F.

Juice 2 zucchini, or enough to make 1 cup of pulp. (If you don't have a juicer shred the zucchini then squeeze it through a cloth to remove as much liquid as possible.)

Add to bowl:

1 cup of zucchini pulp

2 tbsp coconut oil, liquefied

4 room temp eggs (cold eggs will harden the oil)

½ cup honey or agave

½ tsp Cinnamon liquid stevia

1½ tsp ground cinnamon

½ tsp sea salt

¼ cup tapioca flour

½ cup coconut flour, sifted

¼ cup brown rice flour

1 tsp baking soda

1 tsp baking powder

½ cup chopped walnuts

Pour into greased bread loaf pan and bake for about 50 minutes.

One of Andrew's favorite childhood foods was zucchini bread. He asked me to create a gluten-free version, and after a few tries I finally got it. Now it's one of my favorite breads as well!

In about the same time it takes to make one loaf you can double the recipe and make two. After trying it once, I never made a single batch again!

Carrot Cake

Follow zucchini bread recipe. Substitute 1 cup of zucchini pulp with 1 cup of finely chopped carrots. I do this with the food processor. I also like to add raisins.

Unlike zucchini, the carrots should not be strained through cloth and dry.

Banana Bread

Set oven to 350° F.

Add to bowl:

2 mashed bananas

4 room temperature beaten eggs

Cold eggs will harden the oil.

½ cup honey

3 tbsp coconut oil, liquefied

½ tsp Vanilla Crème liquid stevia

½ tsp sea salt

1 tsp cinnamon

¼ cup tapioca flour

½ cup coconut flour, sifted

½ tsp baking soda

½ tsp baking powder

½ cup chopped walnuts

Bake for 50 to 60 minutes.

One thing I think we all have in common is the desire to recreate our mother's banana bread —gluten-free. I have fond memories of eating a warm, fresh slice of banana bread in my childhood kitchen, looking to my mom with such admiration for her cooking abilities. Who knew that baking banana bread qualified mothers as heros? But what was it about that banana bread that I loved so much? I remember… it was soft, fluffy, chewy and sweet. When I began baking gluten-free I couldn't achieve any of those qualities. My first gluten-free banana breads were as dense as lead. Then I started using coconut flour—an amazing, unusual flour. However, the challenge with coconut flour was capitalizing on it's textural abilities, but adding enough flavor to it so that everything didn't come out tasting like coconut and eggs.

This banana bread takes me back to my childhood. It's exactly as I remember it—soft, fluffy, chewy and sweet. I like to top it with ghee and honey, or eat it all by itself. I hope you like it too!

Strawberry Chocolate Chip Muffins

Set oven to 350° F.

Wet ingredients:

3 eggs

⅓ cup honey

¼ cup cashew milk
(see p. 30)
or almond milk *(p. 29)*

1/8 tsp of Vanilla Crème
liquid stevia

**While beating with electric
mixer add:**

½ cup liquefied coconut oil
(So it doesn't solidify from
the cold eggs. Or use room
temp eggs)

Dry ingredients:

1 cup almond meal flour

½ cup tapioca flour

½ cup coconut flour, sifted

¼ tsp sea salt

¼ tsp xanthan gum

1 tsp baking soda

½ tsp baking powder

**Combine the wet and dry
ingredients.**

Add:

1 cup sliced strawberries

½ cup dairy-free
chocolate chips

**Fill unbleached paper cups
almost full.**

*I love the If You Care® brand.
Nothing ever sticks, plus they're
better for the environment and for
my family.*

Bake for about 22 minutes.

Makes about 12.

Quinoa Almond Muffins

Set oven to 350° F.

Add to bowl:

6 room temperature eggs
Cold eggs will harden the oil.

¼ cup coconut oil, liquefied

½ tsp Vanilla Crème liquid stevia

2 tsp alcohol-free almond extract

2 tbsp honey or agave

Beat with electric mixer, then add:

¼ cup plus 2 tbsp almond butter

½ tsp sea salt

½ tsp cinnamon

¼ cup coconut flour, sifted

1 cup Quinoa Flakes

2 tsp baking powder

2 tsp baking soda

Beat again.

Stir in 1 cup chopped or slivered nuts.

Fill unbleached paper muffin cups ¾ full.

Bake for about 15 minutes.

These muffins remind me of corn muffins in taste and texture. They are so good!

Cherry Banana Muffins

Set oven to 350° F.

Add to bowl:

    2 mashed bananas

    4 beaten eggs

    ½ cup honey

**Beat with electric hand mixer.
Then add:**

    ½ tsp Chocolate Raspberry
    liquid stevia

    ½ tsp sea salt

    ¼ cup tapioca flour

    ½ cup coconut flour, sifted

    ½ tsp baking soda

    ½ tsp baking powder

    3 tbsp liquefied coconut oil

Beat with electric hand mixer.

**Fill unbleached paper cups
three quarters full.**

Drop 3 cherry halves on top.

Bake for about 30 minutes.

Makes 12.

Almond Muffins

Set oven to 350° F.

Add to bowl:

½ cup plus 1 tbsp coconut oil, liquefied

½ cup honey

about 12 drops of vanilla crème liquid stevia

3 eggs (I like to beat the eggs in one at a time so they don't heat the oil)

Then add:

2 cups almond meal flour

½ cup brown rice flour

½ tsp baking soda

½ tsp sea salt

2 cups thawed organic cherries, or blueberries, or nuts

Bake for about 24 minutes.

Makes about 14.

There was this adorable cafe where we used to live that always served a pumpkin muffin with their salad. I would feel guilty after eating there though, not because of the gluten—as I was unaware of its effect on me at that time—but because I knew the muffins were not made with healthy ingredients. Now I make muffins like these and I feel good about feeding them to my family. Cheers!

Banana Chocolate Chip Ice Cream

Dissolve:

1 tablespoon of gelatin *(see p. 15)* into ¼ cup boiling water

Set aside.

Add to blender:

3 pitted dates

half a banana

½ tbsp vanilla extract

1½ cups cashew milk

½ cup coconut milk

¼ cup honey or agave

Add dissolved gelatin at the last second, and blend well.

Add 2 tbsp chocolate chips. *I like Enjoy Life®.*

Give it another whirl.

Turn on ice cream machine. Pour mixture into machine.

I was going for extra creamy when I made up this ice cream, and I got it! It's the gelatin which gives this recipe it's creaminess, however, ½ tsp xanthan gum can be substituted if you're vegetarian. I began using gelatin in my recipes because it is healing to the gut, and my youngest needs all the help she can get in that department. We were quite surprised by the fantastic texture the gelatin creates in ice cream. I prefer to add it to all my ice creams now!

Mango Lemon Sorbet

Blend:

3 cups frozen
organic mango

1½ cups sparkling water

¼ cup lemon juice

¼ cup honey or agave

Pour into ice cream machine.

In the heat of the summer, we make my kids'
favorite frozen dessert and it couldn't be simpler to
make.

Coffee Ice Cream

Add to blender:

1 cup of strong coffee,
room temperature or cold

1 cup hemp milk *(see p. 30)*

10 cubes of frozen
cashew milk *(see p. 30)*

1 tsp vanilla extract

¼ cup honey

12 drops of Vanilla Crème
liquid stevia

Just before blending add:

1 tbsp gelatin *(see p. 15)*
dissolved into ¼ cup water
or ¼ tsp xanthan gum

Purée.

Pour into ice cream machine.

Variation:

Add ¼ cup chocolate chips
near the end of the freezing
process.

Blueberry Ice Cream

Add to blender:

- 1 cup frozen blueberries

- 2 tbsp honey or agave

- 3 cups of almond milk

- 1 tbsp gelatin *(see p. 15)* dissolved into ¼ cup boiling water
  or ½ tsp xanthan gum

Blend.

Turn on ice cream machine.

Pour into machine.

Ready in about 20 minutes.

For some reason Zoe, my 6 year old, doesn't like most smoothies, while Ashley loves everything. However, if I take the same ingredients in different proportions and throw them into the ice cream machine—*voila*! She gobbles it up like candy on Halloween. Not that my kids get to eat a lot of candy on Halloween, in fact, I buy their candy from them, and they use the earnings to get toys, but that's besides the point.

So here you go—for breakfast, dessert, or any time in between!

Chocolate Brownie Ice Cream

Dissolve:

1 tbsp gelatin *(see p. 15)*
into ¼ cup boiling water
and set aside
or substitute with
½ tsp xanthan gum.

Add to blender:

½ cup hemp milk *(p. 30)*

2 cups almond milk *(p. 29)*

¼ cup honey or agave

2½ tbsp cocoa powder

**Add gelatin just before
blending.**

Purée.

Add to ice cream machine.

**When it's almost ready add
a cup of crumbled Flourless
Brownies.** *(p. 66)*

Mint Chocolate Chip Ice Cream

Dissolve:

1 tablespoon of gelatin
(see p. 15) into ¼ cup
boiling water
or substitute with ¼ tsp
xanthan gum

Set aside.

Add to blender:

3 pitted dates

1 tsp alcohol-free
mint extract

½ tbsp vanilla extract

1½ cups cashew milk

½ cup coconut milk

¼ cup honey or agave

**Add dissolved gelatin at the
last second, and blend well.**

Add 2 tbsp chocolate chips.
I like Enjoy Life®.

Give it another whirl.

Turn on ice cream machine.

Pour mixture into machine.

Orange Creamsicle Ice Cream

Add to Blender:

3 oranges, peeled and seeded

4 cubes of frozen Vanilla Pudding *(see p. 31)*

1 tbsp honey or agave

1 tsp vanilla extract

½ tsp orange extract
Do not measure over the blender—just in case you spill!

1 cup almond milk or cashew milk *(p. 29, 30)*

Purée. Turn on ice cream machine.

Pour into ice cream machine.

Takes about 20 minutes.

I like to top mine with a sprinkle of cinnamon.

Did you ever have an orange creamsicle or an orange Julius? That's what this ice cream tastes like. I just love it.

Oranges are such a great source of vitamin C. Vitamin C is an antioxidant that helps to protect your body from free radicals which can cause heart disease and cancer.

Vitamin C also produces collagen, which is found in your muscles and bones, and is responsible for holding the cells together.

Cherry Cordial Ice Cream

Add to blender:

2 cups of almond *(see p. 29)* or cashew milk *(p. 30)*

2 cups of frozen organic cherries

2 tsp alcohol-free vanilla extract

2 tbsp agave

about 10 drops of Chocolate Raspberry liquid stevia, or to taste

¼ tsp xanthan gum

¼ cup dairy-free chocolate chips

Blend for a few seconds, just to give the cherries a rough chop.

Turn on the ice cream machine.

Pour into the ice cream machine.

It tastes just like a cherry cordial!

One of my favorite ice cream flavors is cherry. I usually make this recipe with homemade cashew milk, but you can substitute with almond or coconut if you prefer, or use a combination of nut milks.

Cherries are a good source of fiber and vitamin C, and they are also as high in antioxidants as blueberries. Phytonutrients known as flavonoids give cherries their wonderful color and provide a number of health benefits such as the repair of DNA damage caused by smoking and other toxic exposures.

Pumpkin Ice Cream

Add to blender:

1 cup cooked pumpkin
(see p. 59)

¼ cup honey or agave

1 cup hemp milk

¾ almond milk

½ tsp pumpkin pie spice

1 tbsp gelatin *(p. 15)*
dissolved into ¼ cup
boiling water
or substitute with ½ tsp
xanthan gum

Blend.

Pour into ice cream machine.

It took me a couple tries, but this Pumpkin Ice Cream is *really* good. I powered it up with home cooked pumpkin, almond milk, and hemp milk. Hemp milk is a good way to get in essential fatty acids, as well as protein, calcium and iron. I also added a very unusual ingredient, but with good reason—beef gelatin. A while back I made a gelatin dessert after reading that it was healing to the gut. Only I forgot to sweeten it, and therefore my kids refused to eat it. I didn't blame them. Not wanting to waste it, though, I threw some of it into the blender and then made cherry ice cream. The ice cream came out so creamy, like it does when I add xanthan gum—an interesting discovery.

So, still wanting creamy ice cream, and trying to incorporate gelatin to help heal Ashley's gut, I planned to use this method again. First I made the gelatin, the same way as before, then sliced and froze it. Unfortunately, it bonded into a solid block in the freezer, and was impossible to break apart. Next, I foolishly added the gelatin straight to the blender with the other ingredients, without dissolving it first. It separated out against the walls in the ice cream machine.

Finally, I dissolved some gelatin into boiling water before adding it to the other ingredients in the blender. Success! The ice cream was creamy, healing to the gut, and delicious! If someone had told me a year ago that I would create ice cream with beef gelatin, I would have looked at them like they were crazy. Ahhh... the things you do for the love of your children! And creamy ice cream.

How to cook a pumpkin or squash

Put whole pumpkin (butternut or acorn squash) on a dish and into the oven.

You don't need to poke or cut it at all. The fruit will steam itself inside the skin.

Bake for 1 hour at 400° F.

After it cools the skin peels right off, with very little effort.

After peeled cut it in half and scoop out the seeds with a spoon.

Store cooked pumpkin in the fridge in a glass container. Use it for pie, pudding, muffins, and ice cream.

This is my favorite way to cook a pumpkin, butternut or acorn squash. It's so simple, I love it. To illustrate this I took pictures of each step, beginning with when the fruit comes out of the oven, looking a bit prune-like. This was a medium size pumpkin, and it took about 1 hour at 400° F. You know it's done when it's soft to the (glove-handed) touch.

I like to add water to my seeds and let them take about a 6 hour soak, to remove the enzyme inhibitors. Then I rinse them in fresh water and strain (and repeat), before roasting or dehydrating them. This time we roasted them with some coconut oil at 350 for 15 to 20 minutes. When they came out I added sea salt and xylitol—yummers!

See following spread for step by step photos. ⟶

Pumpkin Cookin'

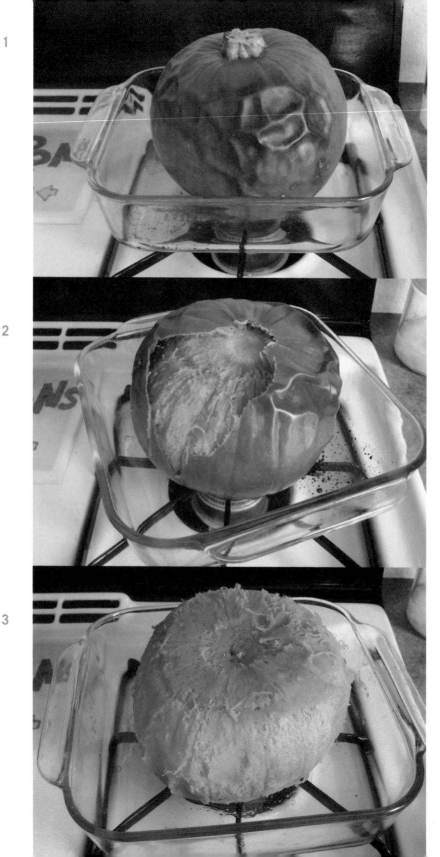

4

5

6

Chocolate Raspberry Cake

Add to bowl:

¾ cup coconut oil, liquefied *(see p. 14)*

½ cup organic cocoa powder

Beat with electric mixer, then add:

¾ cup agave

6 room temperature eggs
Cold eggs will harden the oil.

1 tbsp vanilla

½ tsp Chocolate Raspberry liquid stevia

¼ tsp salt

¼ brown rice flour

¼ cup coconut flour, sifted

¼ cup tapioca flour

½ tsp baking powder

½ tsp baking soda

¼ tsp xanthan gum

Beat again.

CAKE

Pour into greased, floured bundt pan or springform pan.

Bake at 325° F for about 34 minutes.

Top with raspberry jam, Whipped Topping *(p. 32)* **or Coconut Icing.**

CUPCAKES

Fill unbleached muffin cups ⅔ full. Bake at 325° F for about 15 minutes. Makes 18.

COCONUT ICING:

Add to food processor:

½ cup cashews, soaked for about 3 hours, rinsed and strained

½ cup agave

2 tbsp coconut oil

1 tsp vanilla extract

⅔ cup shredded coconut

Purée.

It is amazing to me and my family how little flour is in this cake or cupcakes. That's the joy and wonder of coconut flour. Honestly, no one can ever believe that this recipe is gluten, dairy and sugar free. It's as good or better than any cake I ever had before! Just be careful not to overcook it, and I think you'll agree!

I love the If You Care® brand of unbleached paper muffin cups. Nothing ever sticks, plus they're better for the environment, and for my family. Then, what I do is reuse them by keeping them in a bag in the freezer between use; even better for the environment and my wallet!

Vanilla Toffee Cake

Set oven to 325° F.

Add to bowl:

1 tbsp ghee

¾ cup coconut oil, liquefied *(see p. 14)*

¾ cup agave or honey

6 room temperature eggs
Cold eggs will harden the oil.

1 tbsp vanilla

½ tsp English Toffee liquid stevia

¼ tsp salt

Beat with electric mixer, then add:

¼ cup coconut flour, sifted

¼ cup brown rice flour

¼ cup tapioca flour

1 tsp baking powder

1 tsp baking soda

¼ tsp xanthan gum

Beat again.

Pour into greased and floured bundt pan or springform pan.

Bake at 325° F for about 34 minutes, or until a knife inserted into the middle comes out clean.

For cupcakes bake in unbleached paper cups at 325° F for about 15 minutes.

For presentation you can dust with ground xylitol. This should be done after the cake has cooled fully. Grind the xylitol with a mortar and pestle or in a coffee grinder. Add a scoop of Whipped Topping *(see p. 32)* to each slice.

Flourless Brownies

Set oven to 325° F.

Add to Bowl:

½ cup sunbutter
(for a peanut-like taste)

½ cup almond butter
or 1 cup of almond butter
and no sunbutter, if you
don't want a peanut butter
taste

2 eggs

¼ tsp salt

¼ tsp of vanilla
crème liquid stevia

⅓ cup honey

¼ cup cocoa powder
no more than ¼ cup or
they will be dry

Beat with electric mixer.
If the batter appears too dry add 2
to 4 tbsp of water.

Pour into square greased
cake pan. Spread slightly.
It will even itself out

Sprinkle with ¼ cup dairy-free
chocolate chips. *I use Enjoy*
Life®. I like them because they're
mini.

Bake on the middle rack
for 25 minutes.

For those of you who like the combination of
peanut butter and chocolate, but seek to avoid
peanuts because they carry fungus, this is the
brownie for you. Or if you're not a peanut butter
fan, make them without Sunbutter, for one of the
best brownies ever! Add a little mint and you have
mint chocolate brownies! So many delicious ways to
make them!

Variations:

Chopped walnuts

½ tsp mint extract
(for mint chocolate
brownies)

You can also double the
recipe for a large
rectangular pan. The bake
time is the same.

These are so delicious cold from
the fridge, my favorite way to
enjoy them!

Chocolate Chip Bars

Set oven to 350° F.

¾ cup honey or agave

1 tsp spoonable stevia

1 cup almond butter

1 tbsp vanilla extract

½ tsp sea salt

½ cup coconut oil, liquefied

4 beaten room temperature eggs

Cold eggs will harden the oil.

¼ cup cream of buckwheat

¼ cup tapioca flour

½ cup coconut flour, sifted

2 cups quinoa flakes

1 tsp baking soda

½ tsp baking powder

⅔ cup dairy-free chocolate chips

Beat with electric mixer, then divide into two square, greased dishes.

Bake for about 22 minutes, being careful not to overbake.

I like them best cold from the refrigerator. They also freeze very well.

These bars are so good I could just eat them all day, and why not? The almond butter and quinoa are full of vitamins, enzymes, and complete protein. The coconut oil is a medium chain fat, which converts to energy rather than being stored as fat in your body, and coconut oil is 40 percent lauric acid, which is incredibly anti-bacterial, and anti-viral. Still, they are so delicious, I have to remind myself how healthy they are, so I don't feel guilty eating them for breakfast!

Pavlovas

Set oven to 300° F.

Line a cookie sheet with unbleached parchment paper & very lightly grease it with coconut oil.

Separate 6 room temperature eggs.

Save the yolks in the refrigerator for Custard Pie *(see p. 149)*.

Add the whites to a bowl and beat with electric mixer until they form soft peaks.

Add 2 tsp corn starch, and start beating again.

Slowly add ¼ cup xylitol while beating.

When they are stiff peaks, turn the mixer off and add:

 ¼ tsp Vanilla Crème liquid stevia

 ½ tsp vanilla extract

 1 tsp apple cider vinegar

Gently fold the last three ingredients in by hand with a spatula.

Pile it onto the middle of the parchment paper.

Flatten the top to form about an 11 inch circle.

Put it in the oven for 20 minutes, then turn the temperature down to 250° F.

Bake for another 30 minutes, then turn the oven off.

Keep the pavlovas in the oven for 40 minutes, then remove to cool completely.

You can keep it in the refrigerator if you want to make it ahead, and it will retain its marshmallow texture.

Shown here with Whipped Topping *(p. 32)*.

You can also top it with roasted fruit, like pitted plums and apricots. Roast on a lightly greased pan, cut-side up, at 500° F for about 8 minutes.

Almond Cake with Ganache

Set oven to 350° F.

Add to Bowl 1:

2½ cups of almond meal flour

½ cup brown rice flour

½ tsp baking soda

½ tsp sea salt

Add to Bowl 2:

1 cup coconut oil, liquefied

½ cup honey or agave

1 tbsp vanilla extract

1 tsp spoonable stevia

Add to Bowl 3:

6 egg whites (drop the yolks into bowl 2)

Beat whites to form soft peaks, about 3 minutes with the electric mixer.

Combine bowls 1 and 2 with the electric mixer.

Gently fold in the whites (which are now soft peaks).

Pour into large greased cake pan.

Bake for 25 minutes.

Ganache is usually a 1:1 ratio of dark chocolate and cream, which is made by bringing the cream just to a boil then pouring it over the chocolate. The heat of the cream melts the chocolate and the two are whisked together. This is exactly how I make it, only I use coconut milk, and dairy-free chocolate chips, like Enjoy Life. You can also flavor the ganache with extracts if you like. I add some vanilla to mine. Personally, I think all desserts need a little vanilla!

Coconut Chocolate Chip Cake

Set oven to 325.

Add to one bowl:

¼ cup coconut flour, sifted

2 cups shredded coconut

1 tsp baking soda

1 tsp baking powder

¼ cup dairy-free
chocolate chips

In a separate bowl:

**Beat 6 egg whites to form
soft peaks.**

While beating add:

2 tsp vanilla extract

¼ cup honey or agave

2 tsp coconut oil, liquefied

a pinch of sea salt

**Add whites to dry ingredients
and gently fold together.**

**Pour into greased
8 x 8" dish.**

Bake for about 25 minutes.

What do you do with 6 egg whites left over the day after making custard pie *(p. 149)*? Use them in my coconut chocolate chip cake of course! Whipped egg whites are the secret to making this cake light, fluffy and moist. I've said it before, but we eat dessert for breakfast in my house. I like to make this quick healthy cake first thing in the morning, and serve us a warm, fresh slice. I have some tea or coffee from the French press, and we sit down at the kitchen table to eat, with the morning sun streaming in through the window.

For a dense version don't beat the egg whites to peaks. Good either way!

Blondies

Add to bowl:

2 eggs

¼ tsp of vanilla
crème liquid stevia

¼ cup honey

1 cup almond butter

¼ tsp sea salt

2 tbsp coconut flour, sifted

1 tbsp brown rice flour

¼ cup chocolate chips

2 tbsp coconut oil
or 1 tbsp coconut oil and
1 tbsp ghee
*This should be added as you beat,
so that the cold ingredients don't
harden the oil.*

Beat with hand mixer.

Optional:

1 cup chopped walnuts

**Pour into well greased
square dish.**

**Sprinkle with another ¼ cup
chocolate chips.**

**Bake at 325, for about
25 minutes.**

Waffles

Blend:

2 eggs

2 tbsp ghee *(see p. 14)*

1/8 tsp of Vanilla Crème liquid stevia, or to your taste

one pinch salt

2 tsp tapioca flour

2 tbsp coconut flour, sifted

½ cup brown rice flour

¼ tsp xanthan gum

¼ tsp baking soda

¼ tsp baking powder

1¼ to 1⅓ cups cashew milk *(p. 30)*

Pour into waffle iron, set on high for 3 minutes.

Here is my hand written recipe. I thought you might get a kick out of it. Each time something is scratched out was one try. As you can see it took about a dozen tries! I originally intended it to be pancakes, but it came out better as waffles.

Funa (fake tuna salad)

Soak for at least 3 hours in a lot of water:

1 cup blanched almonds

½ cup raw sunflower seeds

(Sunflower seeds absorb so much water.) Rinse them in a bowl of fresh water and strain. Repeat until the water is clear.

Put them in the food processor and let them purée for about 4 seconds.

Place them in a bowl and add:

¾ cup finely chopped celery

½ cup finely chopped red onion

⅓ cup kosher dill relish

a pinch of sea salt

2 tbsp lemon juice

2 tsp dried dill (or fresh if you can get it)

⅓ cup Vegenaise® grapeseed oil

Optional:

½ tsp ground dried seaweed

This recipe is based on my friend's, Save the Dolphins fake tuna fish. In addition to saving the dolphins there is another enormous reason to avoid tuna. Mercury. According the EPA & FDA mercury consumed by a nursing or pregnant woman or by a young child can harm the developing brain and nervous system. Therefore, they warn not to eat more than 12 oz of tuna fish per week. This, I can only imagine, is *based on the assumption* that nursing or pregnant women, or small children, will weekly be able to excrete small amounts of poison. However, there are those of us who believe there is NO safe amount of poison. Period. Furthermore, not all of us are capable of excreting toxins.

Japanese Inspired Dressing

Add:

¼ cup gluten-free teriyaki sauce*

¼ cup extra virgin olive oil

1 tbsp Vegenaise® grapeseed oil

1 tbsp honey or agave

1 tsp lemon juice

1/8 tsp sea salt

Mix with hand blender.

*I use Premier Japan.
www.edwardandsons.com*

This dressing is inspired by one of our favorite places to eat where we're from. It's a contemporary Japanese restaurant, very cool, great food, and they have an avocado salad with a dressing that tastes just like this. I hope you enjoy it as much as I do.

Spinach Salad

Just wash and dry a bunch of fresh spinach, then lightly sauté in coconut oil. Top with my Japanese Inspired Dressing (above). Delish. I don't know what I love more, the spinach or the dressing. It's also great with avocado on top.

Caesar Salad

(see p. 30)

CAESAR SALAD DRESSING:

Add to a glass container with a lid*:

¼ cup cashew milk, because it tastes like cream *(see p. 30)*

¼ cup Vegenaise® Grapeseed Oil *My favorite.*

1 tsp lemon juice

1 tsp gluten-free teriyaki** *or* worcestershire sauce, *or* 1 tbsp apple cider vinegar

½ to 1 clove minced garlic, depending on how spicy you want it

1/8 tsp sea salt

pinch of pepper

Screw the top on tightly and give it a good shaking.

*I use old almond butter or jam containers.

**I use Premier Japan. www.edwardandsons.com

What did you eat before you knew that you were celiac or casein-intolerant? I used to have caesar salad probably every week, even more before we had children. My friends and I would go out to eat, and caesar salad was my staple dish at restaurants. It comes with lots of nice greens, and the dressing gives it that creamy garlic loveliness. It just makes my mouth so happy. Which is why I made it my mission to create my own caesar salad dressing, and it is delicious! My little salad queen, Zoe, gobbles it right up, even though it's a little, "ficey." I really hope you try it!

Almond & Orange Spinach Salad

Add to blender:

¼ cup orange juice

¼ cup almond butter

¼ cup extra virgin olive oil

¼ cup agave

1 tsp apple cider vinegar

1 tsp gluten-free tamari sauce

Blend.

I just love this salad! Spinach salads are the way to my heart to begin with, but add the almond and orange dressing, the fresh sliced oranges and chopped almonds, plus caramelized onions… I am in taste bud heaven!

Apple Cider Vinaigrette

Add to a glass container with a lid*:

3 tbsp apple cider vinegar

6 tbsp extra virgin olive oil

1 tbsp honey

pinch of sea salt

Screw the top on tightly and give it a good shaking.

This is my youngest, Ashley's, favorite salad dressing. Before I made this she never ate salad, now she can't get enough of it! You can also add a teaspoon of dijon mustard for a great honey mustard vinaigrette.

*I use old almond butter or jam containers.

Corn Chop Salad

For two large (or four small) servings you will need:

- 4 cups of thinly sliced lettuce

- 2 cups of fresh raw (uncooked) corn

Mix with Japanese Inspired Dressing *(see p. 83)*.

Nothing says summer to me more than fresh corn, still in the husk. If you've never tried corn raw, you're in for a real treat; you may never want to cook it again.

Egg Salad

Rough chop 7 hard boiled eggs.

Add to bowl with:

1/3 cup Vegenaise®
grapeseed oil

1/4 tsp Herbamare®
seasoning

2 celery sticks,
finely chopped

1 tbsp finely chopped
green onions

Hard boil 7 eggs. At high altitude I lightly simmer mine (so there are barely a few bubbles) for 10 minutes, then transfer them to an ice water bath before peeling.

Roasted Potato Salad

Chop 6 potatoes into bite-sized pieces.

Roast in coconut oil at 400° F for about 20 minutes, or until tender.

Mix with:

1 handful of
chopped parsley

2 tbsp fresh chopped dill

2 stalks of celery, chopped

1/2 tsp Herbamare®
seasoning

3 tbsp pickle relish

1/3 cup Vegenaise®
grapeseed oil

Potato Skin Fries

Set oven to 450° F.

Skin 6 potatoes with a knife.

Wash potato skins well in a bowl of water and strain.

Lay on a towel to dry.

Add to bowl with:

a few tablespoons of melted ghee or coconut oil

a splash of balsamic

a sprinkle of garlic powder.

Spread evenly on sheet and bake for 15 to 20 minutes.

Top with sea salt, and Old Bay Seasoning®.

Since I don't have a peeler, I skin potatoes (or apples) with a knife. This makes the peels thicker—perfect for making potato skin fries!

Roasted Garlic & Sundried Tomato Dip

Add to processor:

1 head roasted garlic

1 cup cashews, soaked overnight, rinsed well in a bowl of fresh water and strained (do this twice)

¼ cup extra virgin olive oil

1 tsp lemon juice

1/8 tsp sea salt

Purée till smooth.

Add 6 sundried tomatoes.

Purée only a few seconds.

Serve on sliced apples and jicama.

Roast one head of garlic in a small dish with a lid. Let cool. Remove the roasted garlic from the skin.

Creamy Bean Dip

Add to food processor:

½ cup cashews, soaked for 3 to 6 hours, rinsed in a bowl of fresh water and strained

1 cup cooked black beans

1 tsp lemon juice

1 tsp dijon mustard

2 tbsp Vegenaise® grapeseed oil

¼ tsp Herbamare® seasoning

Purée.

Serve on rice thins.

This only makes about a cup and a half. If you are having guests over I would double the recipe.

This is one of those recipes you would be proud to offer anyone, knowing they would never suspect it was dairy-free. It is so creamy and delicious, your guests may think it contains cream cheese. I recommend you serve it room temperature or even warm. If you make it ahead, just take it out of the fridge and put it on the counter a few hours before you plan on serving it, or heat it in the oven for just a few minutes.

I like to make my own black beans, rather than using aluminum cans. It's less expensive, healthier, and if done properly, wont cause gas like canned. First I soak the beans a full 24 hours. Then I rinse them really well in a bowl of fresh water and strain. I do this about 3 times. Next I cook them in a pot with a lid, letting them simmer about 3 hours. Using one of cup beans (measured when dry) I cook them in two cups of water.

Apples with Almond Butter

Apples with almond butter are a healthy treat; good any time, but especially convenient when you're short on time and need a quick snack. Just swirl in some honey and spread it on your favorite sliced apples. The kids eat it up. I also love it on celery sticks.

Spinach and Artichoke Dip

Soak ½ cup of cashews overnight.

In the morning rinse them in fresh water and strain. Repeat about twice.

Add the cashews to the food processor with:

1 tbsp lemon juice

2 tbsp Vegenaise® grapeseed oil

1/8 tsp garlic powder

1/8 tsp sea salt

Purée.

Add:

6½ fl oz glass jar of marinated artichokes, liquid included

10 oz package of frozen organic spinach, thawed, and strained through a kitchen towel to remove as much liquid as possible.

Purée.

I've tried to make this recipe with fresh spinach and it was terrible, so I went back to the frozen. This way is delish.

This dip is quite the crowd pleaser. We spread it on toasted brown rice tortillas, fresh off the dry iron skillet, or smear in on jicama and apples. Yum!

Broccoli Quiche

Set oven to 350° F.

Sauté:

    ½ cup chopped celery

    ¾ cup chopped onion

    2 cloves of garlic, minced

Add to bowl with:

    1 cup cooked brown rice

    2 cups lightly
    steamed broccoli

Mix together:

    3 eggs

    ¾ cup coconut milk

    1 tsp Herbamare™
    seasoning

Combine all ingredients.

Pour into greased 8 x 8" dish.

Bake for 40 minutes.

Zucchini and Tomato Quiche

Set oven to 375° F.

In a bowl beat:

3 eggs

¾ cup coconut milk

¼ tsp Herbamare™ seasoning

Cut a defrosted Gillian's Gluten-Free Pizza Dough in half.

Using flour on both sides, roll out one half, and place it in the greased pie dish.

Layer the egg mixture with the zucchini.

Top with fresh sliced vine-ripened tomatoes.

Bake for 40 minutes.

Lightly saute 1 zucchini, cut lengthwise in quarter inch slices, on each side, in coconut oil or ghee. Let cool.

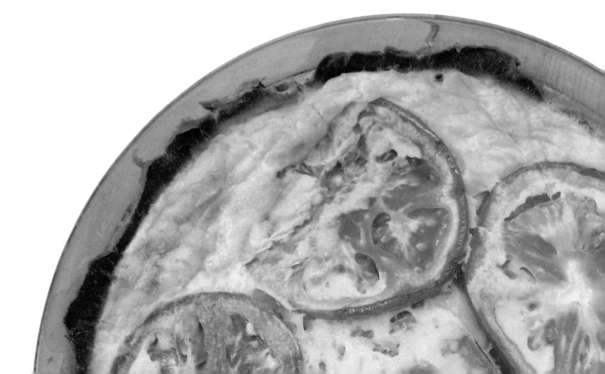

Broccoli Casserole

Set oven to 350° F.

**Saute in 1 tbsp ghee
or coconut oil:**

- 1 cup chopped celery
- 1 cup chopped onion
- 4 cloves of garlic, minced

Add to bowl with:

- 3 cups cooked millet
- 2 cups lightly steamed broccoli
- 3 eggs
- ¾ cup coconut milk
- 1 tsp Herbamare™ seasoning

Pour into greased dish.

Bake for about 45 minutes.

Make 3 cups of millet in your preferred method, or use my technique:

Soak 1 cup of millet in water for a minute. Rinse in fresh water and strain. (repeat two more times) Add to pot with 1 cup of vegetable broth and 1½ cups of water. Simmer, lid on, for about 20 minutes.

Spinach and Artichoke Quiche

Set oven to 375° F.

Lightly saute 5 cups of fresh, cleaned spinach.

Add to bowl with:

¼ cup chives

1 cup marinated artichokes, drained

In a separate bowl beat:

3 eggs

¾ cup coconut milk

¼ tsp Herbamare™ seasoning

Combine all of the ingredients.

Cut a defrosted Gillian's Gluten-Free Pizza Dough in half.

Using flour on both sides, roll out one half, and place it in the greased pie dish.

Pour ingredients over crust.

Bake for 40 minutes.

Green Bean Casserole

Ingredients:

8 cups chopped
green beans

16 oz fresh sliced
mushrooms

3 onions

4 tbsp brown rice flour

4 tbsp coconut oil (or ghee)

2½ cups cashew milk

2 eggs

½ tsp garlic powder

2 tsp Herbamare™
seasoning

4 brown rice tortillas

½ tsp salt

Steam 8 cups of fresh chopped green beans for 10 minutes. *I put them in the fridge to insure they stop cooking, until I'm ready for them.*

Lightly sauté 16 oz of fresh sliced mushrooms.

Caramelize 3 onions in coconut oil or ghee. (make sure there is plenty of oil so they don't burn) Add the above ingredients to a bowl.

To make a rue add 4 tbsp of brown rice flour to 4 tbsp of coconut oil or ghee in a pre-heated pot. Stir.

Whisk in 2½ cups of room temperature cashew milk *(p. 30)*, about ½ cup at a time, allowing it to thicken in between.

Break two eggs into a large glass measuring cup, and temper them with the rue:

Add a splash of the hot cashew milk sauce to the eggs while beating them, to bring them up to temperature without scrambling them. Slowly continue adding the sauce to the eggs while beating.

Add ½ tsp garlic powder, 2 tsp Herbamare seasoning, and a few cranks of ground pepper to the sauce. Combine sauce and veggies. Pour into baking dish.

Toast 4 brown rice tortillas in the oven. Add the toasted tortillas to the food processor in pieces, as well as 2 tbsp coconut oil or ghee, and ½ tsp salt. Purée. Top the casserole with the crumbs.

Bake at 350° F for 40 minutes.

We had this dish at pretty much every holiday in my house growing up, and at no other time of the year. It was always my favorite, my stand-by. If all else failed to be edible, there would always be green bean casserole.

Now that I'm an adult with children of my own, I not only want to serve up this tradition in my own home, but make it healthy. Basically everything in the original is from a can: the green beans, the cream of mushroom soup, the fried onions.

This side dish was unhealthy, cheap and so easy to make. My own version, which rocks my world by the way, has none of these attributes. The amount of processed ingredients in my gluten-free, casein-free version is minimal, and it comes from fresh, local, organic green beans, and onions, and home-made cashew milk. Though it takes some time to prepare, it's well worth the effort, I promise you. I will be making it at every holiday, like my Mom did. Just thinking about my healthy, gluten-free, casein-free version of green bean casserole makes my mouth water!

Penne with Tangy Tomato Sauce

TANGY TOMATO SAUCE:

Add to blender:

10 sundried tomatoes

½ cup of your favorite extra virgin olive oil

3 tbsp balsamic vinegar

1 tsp raw honey

¼ tsp sea salt

¼ tsp garlic powder

Purée.

Tinkyada® is my favorite brand of gluten free pasta. I especially like their brown rice penne with rice bran, which you can find in most health food stores or on Amazon.com. If you're feeling really Italian, try this dish with a nice glass of red wine, and a Dean Martin record. It's always a hit.

Penne with Garlic Cream Sauce

GARLIC CREAM SAUCE:

Add to small bowl:

²/₃ cup coconut milk

¼ tsp sea salt

1 tbsp lemon juice

Preheat pan over low/medium heat.

Add:

1 tbsp ghee

3 cloves of garlic, minced

Allow garlic to get lightly golden, about 3 minutes.

Pour ghee and garlic into liquids.

Mix with hand mixer.
Or use the blender to purée the garlic into the sauce if you prefer.

Pour back into the pan.

Simmer and reduce the sauce for 5 minutes.

Cover pasta with sauce.

Top with artichoke hearts.

The sauce thickens more as it cools.

Using my favorite Tinkyada® penne, I love to add this garlic cream sauce. It's so creamy, no one would ever believe there wasn't any casein, lactose or whey in it. Gotta love clarified butter!

Lasagna

PARBOIL

9 gluten-free rice lasagna noodles for 10 minutes.

The Tinkyada brand are my favorite.

Put them in a bowl of cool water or onto a cookie sheet coated with olive oil to stop the cooking.

"CREAM" FILLING

prepare 2 cups of cream of buckwheat hot cereal, using (full fat) coconut milk

The directions for two servings on the Pocono Cream of Buckwheat box is equal to two cups cooked.

Add to the cream of buckwheat:

½ tsp sea salt

½ tsp garlic powder

1 tsp Italian Seasoning

1 tbsp ghee

After it cools, add four eggs.

Saute:

2 peppers and add them to the "cream" filling or use cooked ground beef or sausage.

Use a 5 qt (rectangular) sized dish.

Layer your noodles with 3 cups of tomato sauce in this order:

tomato sauce, 3 noodles, "cream" filling

Repeat two more times.

I like to put my stainless cookie sheet over top, upside down, because I don't use aluminum. We're trying to get the aluminum out of our bodies here. It does need to be covered, though.

Bake for 45 minutes at 350° F.

Allow to rest for 15 minutes before serving.

I love this recipe so much I like to make two at a time, and freeze one.

It took me several tries to get the gluten-free lasagna noodles to work for me. Some say, "no boiling, oven ready", which is why my first few tries failed. Now I ignore the package instructions and parboil them.

I use a 12 inch wide pan containing a few inches of simmering water to parboil the gluten-free lasagna noodles. I do this in two batches, five noodles and then four.

Also, I am going to pick favorites here, and say that you should really buy Tinkyada lasagna noodles, and not De Boles. Tinkyada, are so much more like semolina noodles, and so much easier to work with.

To create a cheese-like layer, much like the ricotta layer in traditional lasagna, I developed this "cream" filling using cream of buckwheat, and coconut milk, and it is so awesome! It gives you that same texture and creaminess as dairy. Okay, not exactly like dairy, but close!

Butternut Lasagna

CASHEW MILK BÉCHAMEL

Add to pre-heated pot:

4 tbsp of coconut oil
or ghee

I use two of each

4 tbsp brown rice flour

Stir.

Whisk in:

2 cups of room temperature
cashew milk, about ½
cup at a time, allowing it to
thicken in between.

**Break two eggs into a large
glass measuring cup, and
temper them with the sauce
by adding:**

a splash of the hot sauce
to the eggs while beating
them, to bring them up
to temperature without
scrambling them.

**Slowly continue adding the
sauce to the eggs while
beating.**

Add to the sauce:

¼ tsp garlic powder

1 tsp Herbamare™
seasoning

a few cranks of pepper

BUTTERNUT FILLING

Purée:

3 cups of cooked
butternut *(p. 59)*

¾ tsp sea salt

1 tbsp ghee

¼ cup honey
or 2 tbsp xylitol

1½ tsp ground cinnamon

¼ tsp allspice

PARBOIL NOODLES

I use a 12 inch wide pan containing a few inches of
simmering water to parboil the gluten-free lasagna
noodles for 10 minutes. I do this in two batches, five
noodles and then four.

*I much prefer Tinkyada lasagna noodles, over De Boles.
Tinkyada, are so much more like semolina noodles, and so much
easier to work with.*

Layer the lasagna in this order:

béchamel, noodles, butternut filling

Repeat two more times.

Top with remaining béchamel.

Bake covered at 350° F for 50 minutes

*To avoid aluminum going into my food I don't cook with
aluminum foil. I like to cover with my stainless cookie sheet,
turned upside down.*

Soba Noodles with Red Pepper and Sunbutter Sauce

Add to small bowl:

¼ cup coconut oil, liquefied

¼ cup Sunbutter

1 tsp wheat-free tamari sauce

1 tsp wheat-free teriyaki sauce*

1 tbsp honey

Mix with hand mixer.

Sauté in a pre-heated pan for about 5 minutes:

2 tbsp coconut oil

3 red peppers, thinly sliced

½ onion, thinly sliced

Add:

1 clove of garlic, minced

Sauté one minute more.

Add peppers, onion and sauce to rinsed soba noodles.

Toss and garnish with green onions.

*I use Premier Japan.
www.edwardandsons.com*

I use Eden® Selected 100% Buckwheat soba noodles. I recommend you cook them for 7 minutes rather than 8 as it says on the package. After cooking you have to really rinse them well in fresh luke warm water, or they will stick together and become one solid mass. These noodles are different from most gluten-free noodles in that they are nice and soft when eaten cold from the refrigerator.

Potato Soup

**Sauté for five minutes,
in pre-heated soup pot:**

   1½ cup chopped celery

   1 cup chopped onion

Add:

   2 minced cloves of garlic

   Sauté one minute more.

Add:

   5 peeled potatoes,
cut into 1 inch cubes

   5 cups chicken (or other)
broth

Simmer, lid on, for four hours.
*You can also do this in a
slow cooker*

**Mash with potato masher or
purée with hand blender.**

**Add (to taste) ¾ to 1 tsp
Herbamare™ seasoning.**

Sweet Potato Soup

Add to pre-heated soup pot:

   ½ cup chopped onion

   2 cups chopped carrots

   2 cups chopped celery

Sauté about 10 minutes.

Add:

   4 peeled, chopped
sweet potatoes

   3 cups broth

**Sauté with the lid on for at
least 1 hour.**

Remove lid. Add:

   1 tsp Herbamare Seasoning

   1 tsp xylitol

   1¼ cups cashew milk
(see p. 30)

**Mash with potato masher or
purée with hand blender.**

Lydias Stew

Add to slow cooker:

4 cups broth (vegetable or chicken)

4 cups water
Or 2 cups water plus 2 cups coconut milk.

1 cup Lydias Seasoning

½ cup brown rice

5 cups of vegetables like potato, onion, carrots, and celery

or 3 organic boneless skinless chicken breasts, and 2 cups of vegetables

Set for 8 hours low.

Add 1½ tsp sea salt after it's done, but still hot.

Makes 8 servings.

If you use chicken, take it out and shred it with two forks, then return it to the pot. It will shred very easily, and take only a minute.

I call this fabulous soup Lydias Stew, because the star of the show is a cup of Lydias Organics seasoning. I get Lydias Organics at my local health food store, but you can also buy it online. This stew can be made vegetarian or with meat, and it's super simple to make. It's one of my girls' favorites.

<http://www.lydiasorganics.com>

Creamy Pea Soup

Add to blender:

   1 avocado

   1½ cucumbers

   2 cups thawed peas

   2 tbsp lemon juice

   ¼ tsp sea salt

   1 clove of garlic

   1 cup cashew milk *(see p. 30)*

Blend.

Serve with fresh chopped parsley and extra peas.

Vegetarian Chili

The day before:

Soak 1 cup of dry black beans in a bowl with about 5 cups of water.

I soak them for 24 hours.

In the morning:

Drain the beans

Rinse them well in a bowl of fresh water and strain

Repeat a few times

Throw them in the slow-cooker with:

1 qt vegetable broth

I like the Organic Pacific brand

Two 8 fl oz cans of tomato sauce

½ cup brown rice

Set it to 8 hours low.

When it's done add ½ tsp Herbamare™ seasoning.

Optional:

1 tsp hot sauce

Top with sliced tomatoes and chives.

Also great with avocado, black olives or peppers.

Zucchini Thai Soup

Add to pre-heated soup pot:

1 chopped zucchini

1 chopped celery stalk

½ onion, diced

Sauté over medium heat for about 5 minutes.

Add:

1 cup cooked quinoa

½ cup vegetable broth

1 can coconut milk

1 clove of garlic, minced

2 tsp gluten-free teriyaki sauce*

2 tsp gluten-free tamari sauce

Bring to boil, reduce heat and simmer for 5 minutes.

*I use Premier Japan.
www.edwardandsons.com

Roasted Roots with Garlic and Rosemary

ROASTED ROOTS WITH GARLIC AND ROSEMARY:

Add to large rectangular baking dish:

about 10 red potatoes, quartered

2 large or 4 small parsnips, chopped about the same size as the red potatoes

toss in liquefied ghee or coconut oil

Roast at 450 for half an hour.

DRESSING:

Pre-heat small pan over low heat

Add:

a few tablespoons of extra virgin olive oil

4 cloves of fresh garlic, minced

sauté for a few minutes, being careful not to burn the garlic

Remove from heat.

Add:

a few more tablespoons of extra virgin olive oil

1 teaspoon of finely chopped fresh rosemary

½ teaspoon of sea salt

Pour over root vegetables.

For such a low budget dish, these roasted roots with garlic and rosemary taste like they came from a gourmet restaurant! Have them with one of my fresh salads for dinner!

Cider Cabbage and Kale

Add to the slow-cooker:

1 bundle of kale, washed and chopped

1 red cabbage, chopped

2 peeled, seeded granny smith apples, chopped

1 onion, chopped

1 tsp Herbamare™ seasoning

1 tbsp apple cider vinegar

1 tbsp agave

½ cup apple juice or cider

Optional:

1 Polish sausage (Kielbasa), sliced in half inch pieces

Set for 4 hours.

I like to serve mine with a pinch of cinnamon or allspice.

I love coming home to the smell of cabbage and kale cooking in the crock pot. I get such a kick out of that! You just throw everything in and when you get home the house smells like cider. It's so good!

Butternut Soufflé

Set oven to 350° F.

Add to blender:

2 cups of cooked butternut squash

2 tbsp ghee

½ tsp sea salt

¼ cup honey or agave

1/8 tsp nutmeg

1/8 tsp ginger

2 tsp cinnamon

1 tsp vanilla extract

3 eggs

1 cup coconut milk

Purée.

Pour into dish and bake for 50 minutes or until just set.

My favorite way to cook butternut and acorn squash is to put them on a tray in the oven, at 400° F, for about one hour or until they are soft. You don't poke or slice them; just put them in whole. It's so easy.

After they are cool the skin peels right off and you can scoop out the seeds. *(see p. 59 for step by step instructions)*

This pudding can also be made with 2 cups of pumpkin or sweet potato.

Mashed Potatoes

Boil until fork-tender:

1 bag equal to about 5 pounds or 12 large peeled potatoes

Add potatoes to dish with:

¼ tsp garlic powder

1½ tsp Herbamare™ seasoning

a few turns of black pepper

Bring almost to a boil:

1 cup broth

1 cup cashew milk
(see p. 30)

Pour over potatoes and seasoning.

Mash with potato masher or whisk.

Add more liquids if needed.

Many of us would never consider a holiday complete without mashed potatoes and gravy. But how do you get them creamy without cow cream? The secret is cashew milk. Cashew milk is surprisingly like cow cream when added to savory dishes, like my green bean casserole *(see p. 104)* and mashed potatoes with gravy. So go on and give it a try! You will be amazed!

Gravy

Add to pre-heated pot and whisk together:

2 tbsp of brown rice flour

2 tbsp of coconut oil
or ghee

Whisk in:

¾ cups of room temperature cashew milk
(see p. 30)

¾ cups of room temperature broth

Add ½ cup at a time, allowing it to thicken in between.

Whisk in:

1/8 tsp garlic powder

¼ tsp Herbamare™ seasoning

Variation: This gravy can be made with 1½ cups of broth and no cashew milk f̶̶ ̶̶ ̶̶ ̶̶amy taste. Likewise, it can be made with en̶̶ ̶̶ ̶̶ milk and no broth for a delicious cream sa̶̶ ̶̶

Holiday Stuffing

Purée in food processor:

1 loaf of gluten-free bread (about 20 slices), well toasted. *You may have to purée half of the bread at a time.*

Add bread crumbs to a large bowl.

Sauté:

1 diced onion

about 8 oz chopped breakfast sausage

2 large chopped carrots

3 chopped celery sticks

Add to food processor:

sautéed vegetables and sausage

2 handfuls fresh parsley

1 tsp Herbamare™ seasoning

½ tsp poultry seasoning

Purée or pulse to desired consistency.

Add to bread crumbs.

Add:

1½ cups of broth mixed with 2 beaten eggs

Bake in large dish at 350° F for about 40 minutes.

I have made this stuffing so many times and never used the same bread twice. It turns out great every time, no matter what bread you use, because all of the other ingredients add so much flavor. This is one case where you can choose whichever gluten-free frozen bread they have at your health food store, even one you wouldn't eat normally! All my relatives love this recipe, and no one ever guesses it's gluten-free!

As a variation this recipe can also be made with my Quinoa Almond Muffins *(p. 40)* rather than bread. Just substitute the sliced bread with about 15 muffins.

BBQ Beans

Soak:

1 cup organic dry pinto beans for 24 hours.

Rinse well in a bowl of fresh water and strain.

Repeat about three times.

Add to crock pot with:

1 cup water

1 cup juice from BBQ Chicken *(see p. 139)* or use broth

2/3 cup gluten-free BBQ sauce. *I like Bone Suckin' Sauce®.*

1 tbsp mustard

1 tbsp honey

1 tbsp apple cider vinegar

1/2 tsp vegetarian chili seasoning
Be sure it's gluten-free!

1/2 cup finely chopped red onion

Turn crock pot on for 10 hours, low.

Tortilla Pizza

Preheat oven to 450.

Top gluten-free tortilla* with:

extra virgin olive oil

sea salt and garlic powder

caramelized onions

goat cheese

*Substitute vegan cheese
if you don't tolerate goat
cheese.*

tomato

Bake for five minutes.

**I use Food For Life® brand
Brown Rice Tortillas. They are
available at Whole Foods® and
other health food stores, as well
as online.*

It is recognized that cow milk casein strongly resembles gluten on a molecular level. Goat milk, however, is very similar to human milk and contains only trace amounts of an allergenic casein protein, alpha-S1, found in cow's milk.[1] Although many of us find goat and/or sheep milk to be well tolerated and easier to digest, it does not work for everyone.

---

1   "Got Goat's Milk?" Ask Dr.Sears.com. Viewed May 16, 2008.
<http://www.askdrsears.com/html/3/t032400.asp>

Veggie Spring Rolls

SPRING ROLL SAUCE

Add to a glass container with a lid*:

- 1 tsp tamari sauce

- 1 tbsp almond butter

- 2 tbsp sesame oil

- 2 tsp Vegenaise grapeseed oil

- a pinch of garlic powder

*I use old almond butter or jam containers.

For wraps I love to use rice paper. The girls take their positions at the kitchen island and enjoy dropping the rice paper into the warm water. We wait several seconds, then I lift them out and we start to assemble.

The trick is to wrap them as tightly as you can, and keep all the ingredients long. The first time we made them I finely chopped the lettuce and the carrots, so as we ate they fell out. Live and learn!

I dip the rolls, but you can also pour the sauce in before rolling them up.

Chicken Meatballs

Set oven to 350° F.

Add to food processor:

¾ cup almond meal flour

Process to make sure there are no big lumps.

Pour into a large mixing bowl.

Add to food processor:

2 stalks of celery

2 carrot sticks

Process, then add right on top:

4 boneless skinless chicken breasts

a handful of parsley

Process until you have ground meat. *Try not to over-process. Over-processing could make the meat tough.*

Add meat and vegetables to the bowl with the almond flour.

Add:

2 beaten eggs

¾ tsp sea salt

¼ tsp garlic powder

Stir to combine.

Drop tablespoon size onto sheet lined with unbleached parchment paper.

Bake for 25 minutes.

I love bite size food, it's so much fun. We eat these with our homemade sauce in a small dish and chopsticks. It's like eating take out, only much healthier.

This recipe also makes a great meatloaf! Just bake it in a greased loaf pan at 350 for an hour. You can even top it with my homemade tomato sauce!

Homemade Tomato Sauce

Add to blender:

About 4 cups fresh chopped vine-ripened tomatoes.

5 sun-ripened dried tomatoes

2 tbsp extra virgin olive oil

1 tbsp balsamic vinegar

¼ tsp sea salt

1/8 tsp garlic powder

Purée.

Orange Ginger Chicken

Mix in a large bowl with a lid:

1 cup of orange juice

½ cup chicken broth

2 cloves of garlic, minced

¼ tsp Herbamare™ seasoning

1 tsp puréed ginger

Add:

½ onion, finely sliced

4 boneless skinless chicken breasts (one for each person)

Cover and marinate in the refrigerator for about 8 hours.

Add the chicken to a pre-heated pan and pour the onions and liquids over.

Cover and simmer on low heat for about 45 minutes, or until the chicken is no longer pink inside.

Remove the chicken and set it aside. Add:

1 tsp dijon mustard

1 tsp apple cider vinegar

2 tbsp brown rice flour

Whisk and simmer until the sauce thickens.

Serve the chicken over brown rice and top with the sauce.

Chicken Curry

Add to pre-heated pan:

4 boneless skinless chicken breasts

1 cup chicken broth

Cover and simmer about 45 minutes, or until the chicken is no longer pink inside.

Remove the chicken and shred with two forks. Top with Curry Sauce.

CURRY SAUCE:

Combine in a small pot:

½ cup broth

½ cup coconut milk

2 tsp brown rice vinegar

2 to 3 tsp red curry paste
—depending on how spicy you like it.

2 tbsp honey

2 cloves of garlic, minced

1 tbsp brown rice flour

Simmer the sauce and whisk until it thickens.

Chicken Matriciana

Add to pre-heated skillet:

²/₃ cup diced bacon

²/₃ cup yellow onion

Saute until bacon is browned.

Remove the bacon and onion, drain the fat.

Add to the bacon pan:

2 pounds of chicken, seasoned with sea salt and garlic powder on both sides

Put bacon and onions back on top of chicken.

Pour 28 fl oz vine-ripened crushed tomatoes with basil over the top.

Reduce heat to low.

Cover and simmer 45 minutes. Top with fresh basil.

This recipe is made to have left-overs, because it's so good!

Apricot Chicken

Mix together:

  ¾ cup chicken broth

  2 tbsp apple cider vinegar

  2 tbsp honey or agave

Add to pre-heated skillet:

  6 chicken breasts,
  seasoned with Herbamare™

Top each breast with:

  Apricot jam and ½ cup
  chopped dried apricots.

**Pour liquids into pan and
bring to simmer.**

**Reduce heat to low, cover and
simmer about 45 minutes, or
until chicken is no longer pink
inside.**

**Remove the chicken and
set aside.**

Add to liquids:

  2 tbsp of brown rice flour

  1 tbsp dijon mustard

**Whisk over medium heat until
the sauce thickens.** *About 5
minutes.*

**Serve the chicken over brown
rice and top with sauce.**

Swedish Meatballs

Add to food processor:

6 slices of any toasted gluten-free bread

1 roughly chopped onion

2 handfuls of fresh parsley

1 tsp dried rosemary

1½ tsp ground allspice

3 tsp sea salt

1 tsp garlic powder

3 tbsp coconut oil or ghee

Purée.

Add to large bowl with:

2 beaten eggs

¼ cup broth

2 pounds ground beef

2 pounds ground pork

Combine.

Roll into approximately 1½ inch balls and place onto your broiler pan. *This way the fat can drip into the broiler pan and won't splatter all over your oven.*

Bake at 400° F for about 20 minutes.

Makes 75 meatballs.

They freeze wonderfully.

It doesn't take me much more time to make 75 of these delicious meatballs, than it does to make 40, which is why I like to make a huge batch all at once. That way I can have leftovers and freeze half for whenever I need them.

Tip: To reheat these meatballs after they have been in the refrigerator or even frozen, I like to use my steamer pots. This way they don't burn or dry out, but rather they taste as moist and delicious as they did the day they were made.

Tangy Pot Roast

Add to slow cooker:

5 cups of potato,
cut into 1 inch pieces

1 thickly chopped onion

**Poke holes into pot roast
with a knife and stuff holes
with garlic cloves. Season
pot roast with Herbamare
Seasoning.**

**Place roast on top of potatoes
and onions.**

In a bowl combine:

1 cup red wine

1 cup beef broth

1 cup tomato sauce

¼ cup honey

1 tbsp balsamic vinegar

Pour liquids into pot.

**Set to longest setting,
or about 8 hours.**

BBQ Chicken

Add to slow cooker:

1 head of peeled garlic cloves (about 8 cloves)

4 boneless skinless chicken breasts, seasoned with salt

½ cup of water

½ cup of BBQ sauce

Turn it on for 8 hours, low.

Remove the chicken from the pot.

Shred with two forks.
It will just fall apart.

Add ¾ cup more sauce.
Homemade or store-bought, not from the pot.

Save the juice from the pot in the fridge, or freeze. *You can use this juice for my BBQ Beans, p. 129.*

If you are without air conditioning like me, or if you just prefer not to add heat to your home in the summer months, put your slow cooker outside on a covered porch.

Sometimes when I go to the grocery store I stand there looking at the BBQ sauces, thinking about whether or not to make my own. I usually opt to buy my favorite brand. It's called Bone Suckin' Sauce <http://www.bonesuckin.com/>. They are gluten-free, and they don't use high fructose corn syrup. In fact, it's all the same ingredients I would use if I had made my own!

Strawberry Cheesecake

CRUST:

Add to food processor:

¾ cup walnuts and
¾ cup almonds
*The nuts should be soaked for
at least 3 hours, rinsed well in
a bowl of fresh water, and strained.
Do this twice.*

¾ cup dates, pits removed,
soaked for at least 3 hours,
and strained. *Do not soak for
a drier crust.*

3 tbsp cinnamon

Purée.

*Add a couple tablespoons of the
date water if you need to.*

**Using wet fingers, press into
a springform pan, lined with
unbleached parchment paper
on the bottom only.**

FILLING:

Add to food processor:

1 cup cashews
*The nuts should be soaked for
at least 3 hours, rinsed well in
a bowl of fresh water, and strained.
Do this twice.*

Purée with:

1 cup coconut oil, liquefied
*Add a little bit at a time, and let
it purée for a minute in between.*

Next add:

1½ cup coconut milk
Not 'lite'.

½ cup honey or agave

1 tbsp vanilla extract

1 tsp strawberry extract
Taste and add more if you like.

Purée.

Pour into crust.

**Refrigerate at least 8 hours
to reach cheesecake
consistency.**

Add fresh sliced strawberries after it's chilled for about 2 hours. Press them into the filling, or just spread them on top when it's set (in 8 hours).

Makes one very large cheesecake, about 10 servings. For a smaller version, cut all the ingredients in half and use a glass pie dish rather than a springform pan.

Pumpkin Cheesecake

CRUST:

Add to food processor:

¾ cup walnuts

The nuts should be soaked for at least 3 hours, rinsed well in a bowl of fresh water, and strained. Do this twice.

4 pitted dates

1 tbsp cinnamon

Purée to form a ball.

Using wet hands, press into glass pie dish.

FILLING:

Add to food processor:

½ cup cashews

The nuts should be soaked for at least 3 hours, rinsed well in a bowl of fresh water, and strained. Do this twice.

½ cup coconut oil, liquefied

Purée.

Add:

¾ cup coconut milk
Not "lite."

¼ cup honey

½ tbsp vanilla extract

2½ tsp pumpkin pie spice

Purée.

Pour over crust.

Refrigerate for at least 5 hours to form cheesecake consistency.

For a larger version double the recipe and use a springform pan.

Slice thinly and serve with tea. It's very rich and creamy. Freezes well too. Great to have on hand for a surprise visitor.

Key Lime Pie

CRUST:

Add to food processor:

¾ cup walnuts and
¾ cup almonds
*The nuts should be soaked for
at least 3 hours, rinsed well in
a bowl of fresh water, and strained.
Do this twice.*

¾ cup dates, pits removed,
soaked for at least 3 hours,
and strained. *Do not soak
for a drier crust.*

3 tbsp cinnamon

Purée.

**Add a couple tablespoons of
the date water if you need to.**

**Using wet fingers, press into
a springform pan, lined with
unbleached parchment paper
on the bottom only.**

FILLING:

Purée in food processor:

1 cup cashews
*The nuts should be soaked for
at least 3 hours, rinsed well in
a bowl of fresh water, and strained.
Do this twice.*

1 cup liquefied coconut oil
*Add a little bit at a time and
let it purée for a minute
in between.*

Add:

1 cup coconut milk
Not "lite."

¼ cup honey

¼ cup agave

1 tbsp vanilla extract

½ to ¾ cup lime juice
(depending on your taste)

Purée.

Pour over crust.

**Refrigerate at least 8
hours to reach cheesecake
consistency.**

You can also use miniature unbleached paper cups,
which you can fill with this mixture for bite size
key lime mousse. Just keep them cold so they don't
liquefy. They freeze well too. For a smaller pie, cut
all the ingredients in half and use a glass pie dish
rather than a springform pan.

Chocolate Pie

CRUST:

Add to food processor:

1½ cups almonds

The nuts should be soaked for at least 3 hours, rinsed well in a bowl of fresh water, and strained. Do this twice.

¾ cup dates, pits removed

¾ cup dried red sour cherries

1 tsp coconut oil

about 10 drops of Chocolate Raspberry liquid stevia

Purée to form a mass.

Using wet fingers, press into springform pan, lined with unbleached parchment paper on the bottom.

FILLING:

Add to food processor:

4 ripe organic avocados

¾ cup coconut oil, liquefied

Purée.

Add:

½ cup cocoa or cacao powder

½ cup honey

¼ cup agave

1 tbsp vanilla extract

Purée for a few minutes.

Pour into crust.

Refrigerate for 8 hours.

Those of you who are new to raw are probably thinking, "What do avocados have to do with chocolate pie?" or "Eww!" right about now, but have faith! Although it sounds strange, this pie is awesome, and no one would ever know, unless you told them. It's silky and smooth and oh so delicious! I slice it thinly, and freeze it. When company is coming, I take out a few slices to defrost on the counter. They never suspect this pie is different!

This recipe may also be cut in half for a smaller version, using a glass pie dish.

Nutritional value of avocados:
Avocados are rich in good fat, and have 60% more potassium than bananas. They are high in B vitamins, vitamin E and vitamin K, as well as more fiber than any other fruit.

Pecan Pie

CRUST:

Soak 1 cup of cashews for about 8 hours.

Rinse well in a bowl of fresh water and strain.

Repeat about 3 times.

Add the cashews to the food processor with:

1 tbsp ghee

1 tbsp honey

½ tbsp xylitol

1 tsp vanilla

Purée.

Scrape the sides, then add:

½ cup shredded coconut

Purée to form a ball. Using wet hands, press into pie dish.

Cherry Pie

CRUST:
Same as above

FILLING:
Same as above,
but exclude pecans & salt

Add 1½ cups cherries to the crust before pouring in the filling.

FILLING:

Add to bowl:

7 dates, pits removed

7 prunes

1¼ cups of water

Cover and soak for about 8 hours.

Add the dates and prunes, *and their soaking water* to the blender with:

1 tbsp xylitol

1 tbsp ghee

½ tbsp vanilla

¼ tsp salt

2 tbsp Quinoa Flakes

Purée.

Add 1½ cups roughly chopped pecans (lightly toasted if you like) to the filling.

Pour the filling into the pie crust.

Bake at 400° F for 10 minutes. Turn the oven down to 350 and bake for another 10 minutes.

Chill in the fridge for at least a few hours before serving.

Top with my Whipped Topping *(see p. 32)* **or a scoop of dairy-free vanilla ice cream.**

The pie filling is so sweet and gooey, no one would ever believe there was no corn syrup or gluten for thickener! The crust is so light, flaky and delicious! Altogether, the perfect holiday pie!

Custard Pie

Set oven to 325° F.

Add to bowl:

3 eggs

6 yolks

¼ cup honey

¼ tsp salt

Bring just barely to boil:

2¾ cups whole
coconut milk

¼ tsp Vanilla Crème
liquid stevia *Or 2 tsp
vanilla extract.*

**As soon as you see a bubble,
remove from heat.**

**Begin beating the eggs with an
electric mixer on low.**

While beating begin to
slowly pour the milk
into the eggs (so you
don't scramble the eggs).
Continue till all of the milk
is incorporated.

**Pour into pie dish coated
with ghee.**

**Open the oven door.
Slowly place the dish
on the middle rack.**

**Bake for about 30 minutes
or until the custard is just
set in the middle.**

Optional: Sprinkle with cinnamon and xylitol while it's still hot.

Allow to rest on the counter before slicing. Ooh-la-la! Nice cold too.

Chocolate Chip Cookies

Add to bowl:

1 beaten egg

1/8 tsp Vanilla Crème liquid stevia

¼ cup honey

Beat together with a fork. Then add:

1 heaping cup of packed wet almond meal, left over after staining almond milk *(p. 29)*

¼ cup brown rice flour

¼ tsp xanthan gum

¼ tsp baking soda

¼ tsp baking powder

Combine. Then add:

¼ cup chocolate chips
I like Enjoy Life®.

Pat into flat cookie shapes and place onto a sheet, lined with unbleached parchment paper.

Bake at 375˚ F for about 24 minutes.

Variation:

1 tsp cinnamon

chopped walnuts

raisins

After making almond milk *(see p. 29)*, use the leftover wet almond meal from the nut milk bag or cheesecloth to make our favorite cookies. They are so simple and delicious!

Apple Apricot Cookies

Add to food processor:

¼ cup almond butter

1 tbsp xylitol

1 tbsp vanilla extract

¼ tsp sea salt

4 pitted dates

1 tsp cinnamon

⅓ cup apricot jam with no added sugar

I use St. Dalfour.

Purée.

Add to bowl with:

1 cup peeled, finely chopped apples

¾ cup sesame seeds

¼ cup flax seeds

Seeds may be soaked and rinsed first for easy digestion

Mix well.

Coat the mesh dehydrator tray liner with coconut oil, and place it into the tray. Spoon the cookie mixture onto the mesh dehydrator tray liner, using a tablespoon size measurement to drop into cookie shapes.

Dehydrate at 135° F for about 6 hours.

Makes about 20 cookies.

Chocolate Date Cookies

Add to food processor:

7 pitted dates

They should be moist. If they are dry soak them in water until they soften.

½ cup almond butter

4 drops Vanilla Crème or English Toffee liquid stevia

a pinch of sea salt

Purée.

Add:

½ cup shredded coconut

1 tbsp cocoa
or cacao powder

Purée.

Roll into balls about teaspoon size, then press between your hands to flatten. Place onto a dehydrator tray, no liner needed.

Dehydrate at 135 for about 8 hours. Makes about 20 cookies.

Vanilla Cookies

Soak 2 cups of cashews for about 8 hours.

Rinse well in a bowl of fresh water and strain.

Repeat about 3 times.

Add the cashews to the food processor with:

2 tbsp ghee or use virgin coconut oil for raw cookies

2 tbsp honey

1 tbsp xylitol

2 tsp vanilla

Purée.

Scrape the sides, then add:

1 cup shredded coconut

Purée.

Roll and press into shape. Dehydrate for 18 to 24 hours at 130° F.

Optional:

slivered almonds

2 tsp orange or lemon zest

When I made up the crust for my pecan pie, I thought the dough would make a perfect Christmas cookie, like a sugar cookie (I emphasize the word *like* here, as there is no refined sugar in these). Since it's already an almost raw recipe, all that needs to be done is to substitute coconut oil for ghee, and dehydrate. I don't always make these cookies truly raw because I like a slightly buttery taste, so sometimes I keep the ghee. But you can use virgin coconut oil instead, for a raw cookie.

The second best thing to eating these yummy cookies, is the smell they create in your house for 18 to 24 hours (depending on the thickness) while they are dehydrating. It's a cookie dough in the oven kind of smell, only it lasts much longer than baking cookies, and these little guys are packed with nutrition.

See front book cover for a photo of this recipe.

Orange Apricot Clusters

Melt:

½ cup 72% dark chocolate in a double boiler (a bowl sitting on top of a pot of simmering water). Once it is just melted, remove from heat

Add:

1 tbsp coconut oil

2 tbsp honey

1 tsp vanilla extract

1 drop of orange extract

I like to drop the orange extract onto a spoon away from the bowl, just in case. Once I accidentally poured it directly over a bowl and ruined the whole thing.

Stir to combine. Add:

¾ cup slivered almonds

½ dried chopped apricots

Mix the ingredients.

Drop teaspoon sized bites onto a cookie sheet lined with unbleached parchment paper.

Refrigerate.

Once they are solid they can be removed from the cookie sheet and stored (in the refrigerator) in a container with a lid.

Variations:

Coffee: Substitute apricots with chopped, pitted dates, and orange extract with 1/4 tsp coffee extract.

Cherry: Substitute apricots with dried cherries, and hold the extract.

It's really fun and easy making your own "Halloween candy," and much healthier! But if you make these once, you wont be able to wait till October for more! It's nice to know the kids aren't eating candy that's full of refined sugar and corn syrup, which, despite recent commercials, is really bad for you. *(see p. 9 for more on sugar)*

Chocolate Heart Shaped Cookies

Add to bowl:

1 beaten egg

1 tbsp vanilla extract

¼ cup cocoa powder

¼ cup honey

almond meal left over after straining almond milk
(see p. 29)

Mix ingredients.

Using a teaspoon, drop into heart shapes on unbleached parchment paper.

Bake at 375 for about 20 minutes.

Makes about 8 cookies.

These simple but sweet, heart shaped cookies are made with only a few ingredients. The part I love best is that they use the wet almond meal left over after straining almond milk, so there's no waste. It's a great way to use the leftover almond meal. You don't even have to dry it!

Carrot Spice Cookies

Juice about 10 carrots, or enough to get 6 cups of pulp.

Add to the food processor:

about half of the carrot pulp

2 tsp lemon zest
or 2 tsp of lemon juice

1 cup of pitted dates
(about 9 dates)

Process for about a minute.

Add:

the other half of carrot pulp

pinch of salt and pepper

½ tsp ground cloves
*I put whole cloves in
the coffee grinder.*

1 tsp ground ginger

3/4 tsp ground nutmeg

2½ tsp ground cinnamon

½ cup agave

½ cup coconut oil

Process to combine.

Pat into cookie shapes.

Dehydrate for about 10 hours, at 130° F.

When I get my juicer out to make zucchini bread and carrot cake, I take the opportunity to juice carrots for my raw carrot spice cookies. I don't know who loves them more, me or Ashley? They can be as dry or chewy as you want, just start checking them after about 6 hours in the dehydrator, depending on their thickness. Keep in mind that the dryer they are, the smaller they will get, so if you like a crunchy cookie, start oversized. I prefer them dry on the outside and still soft in the middle, which takes about 10 hours for a thin cookie.

Cherry Chocolate Chip Macaroons

Beat 6 egg whites in a bowl with the electric mixer, to form soft peaks.

Slowly add while beating:

½ cup xylitol

1/8 tsp of Vanilla Crème liquid stevia

pinch of salt

Add:

2²/₃ cups of shredded coconut

²/₃ cup chopped dried red sour cherries

¹/₃ cup dairy-free chocolate chips

Fold into egg whites.

Drop tablespoon size onto cookie sheet lined with unbleached parchment paper, trying to form peaks.

Bake on the middle rack at 325 for about 24 minutes. Be careful not to overbake.

Macaroon recipes usually call for refined sugar as well as evaporated milk (which also contains added sugar). I removed these ingredients from my macaroons, but you would never know it, because these little guys are sweet and tasty. They are so good!

Spiced Almond Brittle

Spice mixture:

1 tsp dried ground ginger

1 pinch ground
black pepper

1 rounded tsp ground
cinnamon

1/3 tsp ground cloves

*You won't use all of the
spice mixture in one
batch, but you can save
it for next time.*

In a saucepan bring to boil:

1 cup agave

1/3 cup coconut oil

Add:

1½ cups slivered almonds

½ tsp of the spice mixture

Simmer (so there are little
bubbles) for 20 minutes,
stirring constantly.

Remove from heat.

**Add another ½ tsp of the spice
mixture.**

**Spread on a cookie sheet
lined with unbleached
parchment paper.**

**Place in the freezer
for 2 hours.**

Break into brittle.

Store in the refrigerator.

This brittle is based on a recipe from a book my husband read, *The Medieval Kitchen: Recipes from France and Italy*. He also made me candied orange peel for my birthday once, using another recipe from *The Medieval Kitchen*. It was awesome.

I changed the brittle ingredients notably because it originally called for honey and no oil. I thought that the honey made it way too sweet, and took away from the spices. I also added coconut oil because after Andrew made the recipe from the book it was very soft, like honey with nuts in it. I wanted it to be more brittle-like, although my recipe isn't as hard as a true brittle.

If you kept it in the freezer it would be very hard of course, which is why I take it out after 2 hours and store it in the fridge.

Sesame Bars

Add to food processor:

½ cup honey

¼ cup almond butter

5 pitted dates

1 tbsp vanilla extract

½ tsp sea salt

2 tsp ground cinnamon

Purée.

Add to bowl:

½ cup flax seeds

1½ cups sesame seeds

1 cup sliced almonds

You may soak nuts and seeds first (then rinse) to make digestion easier.

Mix nuts and seeds.

Add puréed ingredients to nuts and seeds.

Mix well.

Lay the mesh dehydrator tray liner on the counter, and coat with coconut oil. Spoon the bar mixture onto mesh dehydrator tray liner. I like to make 6 piles on the liner. Then, using wet hands, pat into bar shapes. Lift the liner onto the tray. *Pressing this firmly while the liner is on the tray could break the tray.*

Dehydrate at 135° F for about 8 hours.

Makes about 6 healthy, scrumptious bars. I like to store them in the refrigerator.

Frozen Sunbutter Fudge

FROZEN SUNBUTTER FUDGE:

Add to bowl:

½ cup liquefied
coconut oil

½ cup honey or agave

1 cup crunchy Sunbutter
(or smooth if you prefer)

1/8 tsp of Vanilla Crème
liquid stevia

½ tsp sea salt

Blend with electric mixer.

**Pour into a large dish or
cookie sheet, lined with
unbleached parchment paper
on the bottom.** *This makes it
thin, which is our favorite.*

Top with:

dairy-free chocolate chips.
I like Enjoy Life®.

**Freeze for 2 hours, slice, and
store in the freezer**

**CHOCOLATE COCONUT
FREEZER FUDGE:**

Add to bowl:

1 tbsp vanilla extract

½ tsp sea salt

1/8 tsp of Vanilla
Crème or English Toffee
liquid stevia

2 tbsp cocoa
or cacao powder

1 cup Almond Butter

¼ cup coconut oil,
liquefied

¼ cup chocolate chips
I like Enjoy Life®.

1 cup shredded coconut

My daughter has struggled with yeast overgrowth in her body, so we avoid peanuts, which grow in the ground and carry fungus (not that this mold is really good for any of us). I came up with this recipe using Sunbutter (sunflower seed butter) because it has a similar taste to peanut butter and everyone loves it. We have made a dozen versions of this healthy frozen treat over the years. Sometimes we add Vitol Egg Protein Powder, and roll it into balls, sometimes we use cocoa or cacao powder and make it chocolate. You can also substitute almond butter or macadamia butter, or add nuts for crunch—be creative!

Chocolate Covered Strawberries

Warm on low till just melted.
Or better yet use a double boiler.

½ cup dairy-free
chocolate chips

1 teaspoon of coconut oil

10 drops of Vanilla Crème
liquid stevia

*Or try Chocolate Raspberry
liquid stevia for a raspberry
version.*

**Dredge strawberries in
chocolate and lay on
unbleached parchment
to dry.**

**Coat half in toasted shredded
coconut.**

Refrigerate.

Indian Rice Pudding

Add to bowl:

3 cans of coconut milk

4 beaten eggs

1 cup cooked
brown rice

½ cup agave

1/8 tsp of vanilla
crème liquid stevia

Bake at 350 for one hour.

I love the crust that forms on top!

Unlike packaged puddings, mine is gluten-free, dairy-free and sugar-free, and you just can't beat that fresh homemade taste. I like it hot or cold, depending on my mood, and the weather. Top with cinnamon and organic golden raisins, which have been soaked for an hour to make them plump and moist. You could also add the raisins to the recipe and bake them in the dish.

This recipe is for a big batch, because I like to have lots of leftovers.

Granola

Soak 4 cups of nuts and seeds.

I like to use 1 cup each of almonds, cashews, walnuts and sunflower seeds, and let them soak about 5 hours.

Rinse them really well in a bowl of fresh water and strain. Repeat several times.

Add ground spices to a small glass or dish:

1 tbsp cinnamon

1 tsp ginger

1/8 tsp nutmeg

1/8 tsp cloves

½ tsp sea salt

Add to large bowl:

2 tbsp coconut oil, liquefied

2 tbsp honey or agave

Mix together oil and sweetener.

Add the nuts to the bowl.

Pour the spice mixture over the nuts and stir to combine all the ingredients.

Dehydrate *(p. 15)* **for 12 to 24 hours, until the nuts are completely dry.**

You can layer the granola with fresh fruit and vanilla pudding *(p. 31)* or add dried fruit to the granola and eat it by the handful. Store granola in the refrigerator.

Nuts contain an enzyme inhibitor which makes them hard to digest. By soaking them (and rinsing them well in fresh water) you are removing this enzyme inhibitor, making them easier to digest, and giving your body access to all the nutrition available in nuts. *(see page 14 for information on dehydrators)*

Bananas Foster

Preheat pan on medium heat.

Cut a banana into half inch pieces. *If the pieces are too thin they may fall apart or turn to mush.*

Add to the pan:

1 tsp of coconut oil
1 tsp of ghee

Or two teaspoons of either, but ghee gives it that buttery flavor, minus the casein and lactose.

Fry banana slices on each side for a couple of minutes so they get nicely browned.

Sprinkle with:

a pinch of sea salt

a few pinches of xylitol.

Add to bowl of Vanilla Pudding *(see p. 31)*.

Here's the thing about eating healthy: You can even have dessert for breakfast! This is one of my favorite breakfast foods. It's a little different from the one they serve in restaurants (there's no sugar, alcohol, casein or lactose), but it's just as delicious— I promise!

Recommended Reading

FAVORITE WEBSITES

Generation Rescue <http://www.generationrescue.org/>

Know Shots <http://www.knowshots.com/>

Dr. Joseph Mercola <http://www.mercola.com/>

Shoot Em Up The Documentary <http://www.shootemupthedocumentary.com/>

BOOKS

Bock, Kenneth and Stauth, Cameron. *Healing the New Childhood Epidemics: Autism, ADHD, Asthma, and Allergies: The Ground-breaking Program for the 4-A Disorders.* Ballantine Books, 2008.

Kirby, David. *Evidence of Harm,* St Martin's Griffin, 2005.

McCandless, Jaquelyn. *Children with Starving Brains: A Medical Treatment Guide for Autism Spectrum Disorder.* Bramble Books, 2007.

McCarthy, Jenny. *Louder Than Words: A Mother's Journey in Healing Autism.* Plume, 2008.

Smith, Melissa. *Going Against the Grain: How Reducing and Avoiding Grains Can Revitalize Your Health.* McGraw-Hill, 2002.

SUPPLEMENTS for AUTISM SPECTRUM DISORDER

Zyme Prime™ by Houston, Cal/Mag Citrate by New Beginnings Nutritionals, Awaken™ Nutrition Liquid Vitamins and Minerals, CellFood by NuScience Corporation, Berry Frutol by Pharmax, HLC Mindlinx by Pharmax, Klaire Labs Probiotics, Acai Emergen-C® by Alacer Corp.

Metric Conversion Tables

Temperature

Fahrenheit	=	Celsius
200–205	=	95
220–225	=	105
245–250	=	120
275	=	135
300–305	=	150
325–330	=	165
345–350	=	175
370–375	=	190
400–405	=	205
425–430	=	220
445–450	=	230
470–475	=	245

English to Metric Formulas

Liquid

teaspoons (tsp)	x	5.0	= milliliters
tablespoons (tbsp)	x	15.0	= milliliters
fluid ounces (fl oz)	x	30.0	= milliliters

Weight

cups	x	0.24	= liters
ounces (oz)	x	28.0	= grams
pounds	x	0.45	= kilograms

Common Liquid Measurements

1/8 teaspoon (tsp)	=	0.625	milliliters
¼ tsp	=	1.25	ml
½ tsp	=	2.50	ml
⅔ tsp	=	3.30	ml
¾ tsp	=	3.75	ml
1 tsp	=	5.00	ml
1¼ tsp	=	6.25	ml
1½ tsp	=	7.50	ml
1¾ tsp	=	8.75	ml
2 tsp	=	10.00	ml
1 tablespoon (tbsp)	=	15.00	ml
2 tbsp	=	30.00	ml
¼ cup	=	.06	liters
½ cup	=	.12	l
⅔ cup	=	.15	l
¾ cup	=	.18	l
1 cup	=	.24	l
1¼ cups	=	.30	l
1½ cups	=	.36	l
1⅔ cups	=	.40	l
2 cups	=	.48	l
2½ cups	=	.60	l
2⅔ cups	=	.64	l
3 cups	=	.72	l
3½ cups	=	.84	l
4 cups	=	.96	l
4½ cups	=	1.08	l
5 cups	=	1.20	l
5½ cups	=	1.32	l

Index

Smoothies & Shakes

Chocolate Shake, 19

Mint Shake, 20

Nutcracker Sweet Tea Latté, 21

Purple Pear Smoothies, 23

Chocolate Banana Shake, 24

Cherry Smoothie, 24

Power Smoothie, 25

Blueberry Cream Smoothie, 25

Frozen Café au Lait, 27

Nut Milk & Pudding

Almond Milk, 29

Cashew Milk, 30

Hemp Milk, 30

Vanilla Pudding, 31

Chocolate Mousse, 31

Whipped Topping, 32

Bread & Muffins

Pumpkin Muffins, 34

Zucchini Bread, 36

Carrot Cake, 36

Banana Bread, 38

Strawberry Chocolate Chip Muffins, 39

Quinoa Almond Muffins, 40

Cherry Banana Muffins, 42

Almond Muffins, 44

Ice Cream

Banana Chocolate Chip Ice Cream, 47

Mango Lemon Sorbet, 48

Coffee Ice Cream, 48

Blueberry Ice Cream, 49

Chocolate Brownie Ice Cream, 51

Mint Chocolate Chip Ice Cream, 53

Orange Creamsicle Ice Cream, 54

Cherry Cordial Ice Cream, 55

Pumpkin Ice Cream, 57

Pumpkin Cookin'

How to Cook a Pumpkin or Squash, 59

Cakes & Brownies

Chocolate Raspberry Cake, 62

Vanilla Toffee Cake, 64

Flourless Brownies, 66

Peanut-like Brownies, 66

Mint Chocolate Brownies, 66

Chocolate Chip Bars, 68

Pavlovas, 70

Almond Cake with Ganache, 72

Coconut Chocolate Chip Cake, 74

Blondies, 76

Waffles, 78

Salad & Appetizers

Funa (fake tuna salad), 81

Spinach Salad, 83

Japanese Inspired Dressing, 83

Caesar Salad, 85

Almond & Orange Spinach Salad, 86

Apple Cider Vinaigrette, 86

Corn Chop Salad, 87

Egg Salad, 88

Roasted Potato Salad, 88

Potato Skin Fries, 89

Roasted Garlic &
Sundried Tomato Dip, 91

Creamy Bean Dip, 93

Apples with Almond Butter, 95

Spinach & Artichoke Dip, 97

Quiche & Casserole

Broccoli Quiche, 98

Zucchini & Tomato Quiche, 100

Broccoli Casserole, 101

Spinach & Artichoke Quiche, 102

Green Bean Casserole, 104

Pasta

Penne with Tangy Tomato Sauce, 107

Penne with Garlic Cream Sauce, 109

Lasagna, 110

Butternut Lasagna, 112

Soba Noodles with Red Pepper &
Sunbutter Sauce, 113

Soup

Potato Soup, 114

Sweet Potato Soup, 114

Lydias Stew, 115

Creamy Pea Soup, 116

Vegetarian Chili, 118

Zucchini Thai Soup, 120

Sides

Roasted Roots with
Garlic & Rosemary, 123

Cider Cabbage & Kale, 124

Butternut Soufflé, 125

Mashed Potatoes, 126

Gravy, 127

Holiday Stuffing, 128

BBQ Beans, 129

Tortilla Pizza, 130

Veggie Spring Rolls, 131

Meat

Chicken Meatballs, 133

Homemade Tomato Sauce, 133

Orange Ginger Chicken, 134

Chicken Curry, 135

Chicken Matriciana, 135

Apricot Chicken, 136

Swedish Meatballs, 137

Tangy Pot Roast, 138

BBQ Chicken, 139

Pie & Cheesecake

Strawberry Cheesecake, 141

Pumpkin Cheesecake, 142

Key Lime Pie, 143

Chocolate Pie, 145

Pecan Pie, 147

Cherry Pie, 147

Custard Pie, 149

Cookies & Treats

Chocolate Chip Cookies, 150

Apple Apricot Cookies, 152

Chocolate Date Cookies, 153

Vanilla Cookies, 154

Orange Apricot Clusters, 155

Coffee Clusters, 155

Cherry Clusters, 155

Chocolate Heart Shaped Cookies, 156

Carrot Spice Cookies, 158

Cherry Chocolate Chip
Macaroons, 160

Spiced Almond Brittle, 162

Sesame Bars, 164

Frozen Sunbutter Fudge, 166

Chocolate Coconut Freezer Fudge, 166

Chocolate Covered Strawberries, 168

Indian Rice Pudding, 170

Granola, 171

Bananas Foster, 172

Notes

Notes

Notes

Made in the USA
Lexington, KY
05 December 2010